Claudio Pescio

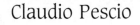

THE UFFIZI

Gallery Tour

FOLD-OUT GROUND PLAN FOR THE IMMEDIATE IDENTIFICATION
OF ALL THE WORKS AND THEIR EXACT LOCATION

384 COLOUR ILLUSTRATIONS

1992-93 EDITION

BONECHI-EDIZIONI «IL TURISMO»
FIRENZE

Photographs: Bonechi archives
Editing, lay-out and cover: Piero Bonechi and Rolando Fusi
Coordination: Simonetta Giorgi
Translation: Rosalynd Pio
Colour separation: La Fotolitografia, Florence
Typesetting: Leadercomp, Florence
Printing: Lito Terrazzi, Florence

ISBN 88-7204-036-1

© Copyright by Bonechi - Edizioni «Il Turismo» s.r.l.
Via dei Rustici, 5 - 50122 Firenze
Tel. (055) 2398224/5 - Fax (055) 216366
Printed in Italy,

The Uffizi Loggia in an old print at the Museum of Firenze com'era.

HISTORY OF THE UFFIZI

Towards the middle of the 16th century, Grand Duke Cosimo I de' Medici commissioned a building capable of containing all the administrative offices of the grandduchy. It was called «Uffizi» (offices), a name that would remain long after the office building had been turned into a museum. In 1559, Giorgio Vasari, painter, art historian, and one of the most prominent architects and townplanners of his day, received the commission for the project. All the houses on the plot of land between Piazza della Signoria and the Arno River were bought up and the vast area became the building site. Parts of the 11th century church of San Piero Scheraggio were actually incorporated into the structure as it was going up and today remains of the apse are still visible (both outside, along Via della Ninna, and inside the museum). Vasari's plan also included a ½ mile long, covered passageway linking Palazzo Vecchio with Palazzo Pitti. By the time the main structure was almost completed (1565) the *Vasari Corridor* which passes over Ponte Vecchio and spans Via della Ninna by means of an overhead bridge, was also on its way to completion. Vasari's three-sided building incorporating a ground-floor arcade encloses a kind of elongated courtyard, the *Piazzale degli Uffizi*. At the far end, the arches open out onto the Arno, beautifully framing the superb view. The architecture of the exterior is the traditional Florentine juxtaposition of white plaster and grey *pietra serena* (sandstone) that contrast so strikingly with each other and create a succession of alternating geometrical voids and volumes. Vasari's plan for the Uffizi was strongly influenced by Michelangelo's Laurentian Library designed in 1524. The architectural themes used by Michelangelo, both in the New Sacristy, as well as in the Laurentian Library are re-used by Vasari on the outside of the Uffizi. Interestingly enough, while Vasari was inserting a new, wholly 16th century style structure into the medieval fabric of the center of Florence, he took great pains not to disturb the harmony of the 13th century civic centre. In fact, one of his chief aims was to create a kind of architectural backdrop for Palazzo Vecchio towering by the Uffizi. In 1580 when Cosimo's successor, Francesco I, an art connoisseur and amateur scientist, decided to restructure the loggia on the top floor of the building creating rooms for his art collections, scientific curiosities, and laboratories, he called in a well-known architect, Bernardo Buontalenti. Buontalenti started work on two projects simultaneously: the Grandducal Theater on the second floor, where the Prints and Drawings Collection is today, and the *Tribuna* on the third floor, designed as a showplace for the Medici's most precious treasures. By 1586 the rebuilding was practically finished. A great number of works in Palazzo Vecchio and Palazzo Medici which had been collected

3

by Cosimo the Elder, Lorenzo the Magnificent, and Francesco's father, Cosimo I, were arranged in the new halls. This basic collection, which included masterpieces by Botticelli, Paolo Uccello, and Filippo Lippi, grew over the centuries, thanks to the interest taken in it by Francesco I's successors. Ferdinando I ordered all the works stored in the Villa Medici in Rome removed to the Uffizi. In 1631 Ferdinando II added the great Urbino legacy, inherited by his wife Vittoria della Rovere from her parents, the last Duke and Duchess of Urbino, which included Piero della Francescas, Titians, and Raphaels. In 1675 Cardinal Leopoldo de' Medici added his collection of several portraits and the first group of drawings. Cosimo III collected gemstones, medals, and coins, and had famous Classical sculptures such as the celebrated *Medici Venus*, the *Scythian sharpening his Knife*, and the *Wrestlers*, among others, brought up from Rome. Anna Maria Lodovica, the Electress Palatine and last of the dynasty, not only added Flemish and German paintings, but in 1743 also bequeathed the whole collection to Florence on the condition that all the works remain in the town. The Hapsburg Lorraine Grand Dukes followed in the Medici's footsteps: Franz-Stefan (Francesco II) gave antique sculptures and coins. Pietro Leopoldo, not only installed the Medici treasures in Florence and Rome, in the Uffizi, but was also responsible for the restructuring of a special hall in the Uffizi for the *Niobe and her children* he had had conveyed from Villa Medici in Rome in 1780. Last but not least, Pietro Leopoldo had the gallery rearranged according to modern museum ideas and had it opened to the public. In the 19th century, several specialized museums, such as the Archeological Museum, the Bargello National Museum, and the Fra Angelico (San Marco) Museum, were opened in Florence, abstracting a number of works from the Uffizi Gallery. Part of the building was used for the State Archives (1852) and at the end of the century, the theater was dismantled to make room for other halls. In the mid - 1800s niches were cut into the arcade columns facing onto the central courtyard and statues of famous Tuscans, sculpted by prominent sculptors such as Giovanni Dupré and Lorenzo Bartolini, were placed inside them. Two innovations were introduced in the present century: after years of being closed to the public the *Vasari Corridor* was re-opened. It contains a ½ mile long exhibition of 17th and 18th century paintings, as well as the famous Uffizi self-portrait collection. Secondly, the Uffizi now has an Educational Department, the staff of which organise guided tours for schools and helps work-out study plans.

The Uffizi Loggia seen from Palazzo Vecchio during the annual flower show.

Above: **The Uffizi Loggia overlooking the Arno, with the beginning of the Vasari Corridor on the left;** *below*: **four members of the Medici family who played a decisive rôle in the creation of the Uffizi Gallery.**

Cosimo I, son of Giovanni delle Bande Nere (Medici cadet branch), condottiero (war leader) and of Maria Salviati, grand-daughter of Lorenzo the Magnificent. Able politician, and disposing of a strong army, he brought Tuscany under the sway of the Medici.

Francesco I, succeeded his father Cosimo as Grand Duke of Tuscany. He was reserved and preferred art and alchemy to governing the state. His second wife was Bianca Cappello; both died in 1597 at Poggio a Caiano at a few hours distance from each other.

Cosimo III, unlike his father, Ferdinand II, was bigoted and indolent, he was also badly advised and persecuted both Jews and Protestants. His wife Marguerite Louise d'Orléans, cousin to Louis XIV detested him and took refuge in a convent in Paris.

Anna Maria Ludovica, last of her line, was sister to Gian Gastone; a great art lover, she left all the grandducal collections to her beloved Florence. While married to Johann Wilhelm of Neuburg, Elector Palatine, she lived at his court in Düsseldorf.

Above: **apse of San Piero a Scheraggio**; *below*: **Dante Alighieri.**

REMAINS OF SAN PIERO SCHERAGGIO

Leading out of the entrance hall where tickets are sold are two recently-restored rooms that were once part of San Piero Scheraggio. The church, built above a still older 9th century one, was consecrated in 1068. In 1292, when it served as the seat of the Councils of the Commune, Giano della Bella issued his Orders of Justice regarding the administration of the city within these walls, while Dante and Boccaccio spoke from the church pulpit. When the church was incorporated into the Uffizi building in 1560, it was drastically restructured, although services continued to be held inside up to the mid - 1700s. In the first room beneath a raised platform, the remains of the original flooring and several medieval tombstones are visible. Andrea del Castagno's frescoes of illustrious men are temporarily hung around the walls: *the Cumaean Sibyl, Giovanni Boccaccio, Petrarch, Dante Alighieri, Farinata degli Uberti, Pippo Spano, Niccolò Acciaiuoli, Esther* and *Queen Tomiri.* These statuesque figures possess the same heroic quality that the artist always gave his human figures (such as his famous mounted *Niccolò da Tolentino* frescoed some years later in the Cathedral of Santa Maria del Fiore). The great panel of the *Battle of San Martino*, by Corrado Cagli, and donated to the Uffizi by Franco Muzzi hangs on the right wall. In the second room, there are several fragments of the original fresco decoration still visible in the apse window embrasures and on the walls. See also: the *Madonna of the Ninna*, by the Master of San Martino alla Palma (14th cent.). In the lobby (cloakroom and lifts), flanking the doorway, are two columns from the right aisle of San Pietro Scheraggio, with traces of their original fresco decoration (on one, a figure of St. Francis is visible). A portrait of Anna Maria Ludovica de' Medici, Electress

Queen Tomiri
Petrarch

Pippo Spano
Giovanni Boccaccio

The Cumaean Sybil
Farinata degli Uberti

Above: **study of two heads, by Leonardo da Vinci; sketch of Pallas, by Botticelli;** *below*: **sketch of a landscape, by Leonardo da Vinci;** *opposite*: **study of a man's head, by Michelangelo** (Prints and Drawing Collection).

Palatine, who bequeathed the Uffizi to Florence, hangs opposite above a bronze group (Archeology) by Giorgio De Chirico. Opposite the lifts, up some steps, a frescoed *Annunciation* by Botticelli, from the Monastery of San Martino alla Scala, considered one of the Sandro's best pieces.

VASARI'S STAIRCASE AND THE PRINTS AND DRAWINGS COLLECTION

Greek and Roman statues and busts, as well as sculpture of other periods have been placed all the way up the great staircase by Giorgio Vasari leading to the upper floors. Off the second floor landing (left side) is the entrance to the **Prints and Drawings Collection** (*Gabinetto dei Disegni e Stampe*). This unique collection was started by Cardinal Leopoldo de' Medici in 1675. It was housed in Palazzo

Pitti, until Cosimo III had it moved to the Uffizi and arranged by Filippo Baldinucci. In the 18th century it was moved to the Buontalenti «Tribuna». Later, as the collection increased, it was moved to other rooms and was given its final home in the rooms built in what had formerly been the Medici theatre designed by Buontalenti (dismantled in the 19th cent.). The collection was greatly enlarged thanks to acquisitions and bequests, and today totals over 50,000 drawings and 60,000 prints, by Italian and non-Italian artists such as Leonardo da Vinci, Michelangelo, Paolo Uccello, Fra Angelico, Pietro da Cortona, Rubens and a host of other well-known names.The first room is used for special exhibitions, often of considerable interest. Only authorized scholars may use its special services which include a photolibrary and an iconographic file.

FIRST CORRIDOR

Originally, the three corridors were a single loggia open on the side facing into the Piazzale degli Uffizi. In 1580, Buontalenti restructured the upper floor, giving it its present appearance and a large group of artists, including Bachiacca, commenced painting the splendid grotesque decoration frescoed on the ceilings. The tapestries that used to hang on the left wall are 16th century. Those depicting the months of the year and the grotesque motifs, were produced in Florence after designs by Bachiacca. The othes, showing festivities at the court of Henri III and Catherine de' Medici, are Flemish. They have recently been removed to be cleaned and restored. Due to the excessive sunlight and heat they are exposed to during the summer months, they will probably he hung elsewhere in future. Along the top of the wall is a series of portraits of historic figures from the Gioviana Collection (16th-18th centuries). On either side of the gallery are Roman sculptures. The highlights include the group of *Hercules slaying the Centaur* at the beginning of the hall, a statue of *Persephone* (Roman copy of a 4th century B.C. Greek original), an *Apollo* (copy of an original by Praxiteles), and several Roman sarcophagi carved in high and low relief dating from the Imperial period.

Above: **The last flight of the great Vasari staircase;** *below*: **the vestibule at the entrance to the Gallery.**

Above: the first corridor seen from the entrance, looking south; *below*: Herakles wrestling with a centaur, Hellenistic; Pompeius Magnus, Roman, Ist century B.C.; bust of Agrippa, Roman, Ist century B.C.

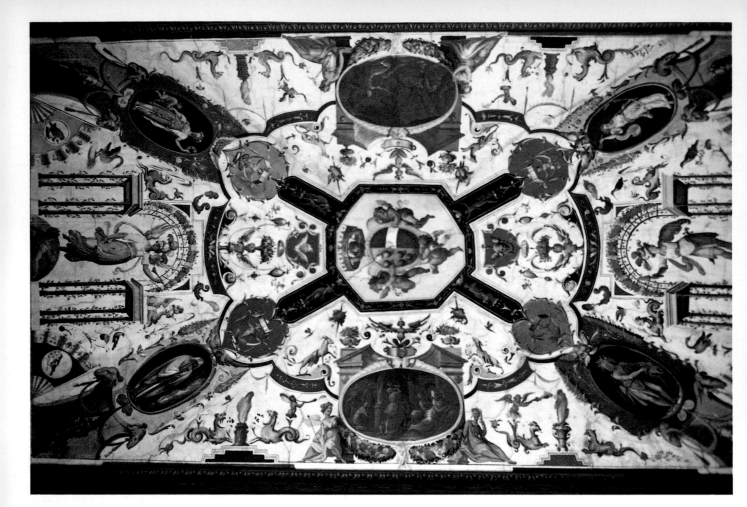

Above: **detail of the ceiling in the first corridor;** *below*: **bust of unknown, Roman, Ist century A.D.; Domitia, Roman, Ist century A.D.; bust of unknown, Roman, 2nd century A.D. (First Corridor)**

Above: **detail of the ceiling in the first corridor**; *below*: **Marciana, Roman, 2nd century A.D.; Hadrian, Roman 2nd century A.D.; Nerva, Roman, Ist century A.D.** (First Corridor)

IF ONE WISHES TO IDENTIFY THE ROOM IN WHICH A WORK HAS BEEN PLACED AND IF ONE WANTS TO HAVE AN OVERALL VIEW OF THE MUSEUM, SEE THE FOLD-OUT TABLE AT THE END OF THE BOOK. THE WORKS IN EACH ROOM ARE DESCRIBED FROM RIGHT TO LEFT, I.E.: ANTICLOCKWISE.

ROOM 1
(Classical Sculpture)

The main nucleus of the Uffizi classical sculpture collection was assembled by the Medici family during the second half of the 16th century. Cosimo I's passion for Roman art was partly due to his desire to create a parallel between Imperial Rome and the Grandduchy of Tuscany. The Hapsburg-Lorraine family continued to add to the collection, which includes a large number of Roman originals of excellent quality and Imperial Roman copies of Greek orginals. Room 1 recently re-opened, used to contain the original panels of the Ara Pacis, which were transferred to Rome in the 1920s, when the Ara Pacis was reconstructed.

Crysippus, Roman copy of Hellenistic original

Ara Pacis, Sacred Procession (cast of the Augustean original).

Labours of Hercules, Roman (2nd century A.D.).

Demosthenes, Roman copy from Greek original (4th cent. B.C.).

Sacrifice of Aeneas, Renaissance relief in Roman style.

Relief with Maenads, Roman copy of Greek original (5th century B.C.).

Relief with Temple of Vesta, Roman (2nd century A.D.).

Propitiatory dance to Marine deity, Roman art (3rd century A.D.).

Torso of the Spearman by Policletus, Roman copy of 5th century Greek original.

Relief of the «Nike Athene balustrade» type, Roman copy of Greek original (5th century B.C.).

Fragmentary relief with two-wheeled chariot, Greek (4th century B.C.)

Cushion Merchant's shop, Roman (1st century A.D.)

Alkibiades, Roman copy of Greek original (4th cent. B.C.).

Copy of the 5th cent. B.C. Spearman by Policletus, Roman copy of Greek original.

Sacrifical Scene, Roman (2nd century A.D.)

Seated Wayfarer, Roman (2nd century A.D.)

Lamentation over a dead boy, Roman (2nd century A.D.)

Copy of the 5th century Spearman by Policletus, Roman copy of Greek original.

Cloth Merchant's Shop, Roman (1st century A.D.)

Unknown, Roman (3rd century A.D.)

Above: **parastas, Roman, 1st century A.D.**; *below*: **Philosopher's bust, Roman copy of Greek original.**

Above: **Roman copy of Greek 5th century B.C. Spearman, by Policletus; overall view of the Classical Sculpture Room;** *below*: **the Labours of Herakles, Roman, 2nd century A.D.**

Seated Wayfarer, Roman, 2nd century A.D.

Dancing Horaï – Neo-Attic (2nd/1st century B.C.)

ROOM 1 continued

Cherub with bolt of lightning, Imperial Roman period.

Mark Anthony, Roman (1st century A.D.)

Ara Pacis, Allegory of Earth, Air and Water (plaster cast of the original).

Parastas, (decorated pilaster) - Roman (1st cent. A.D.)

Cicero, Roman (1st century A.D.)

Cherubs with breast-plate, Roman (2nd century A.D.)

Philosopher, Roman copy of Greek original.

Propitiatory dance to Marine deity, Roman art (2nd century A.D.).

Dancing Horaï, Neo-Attic (2nd/1st B.C.)

Ara Pacis, Sacred procession with Augustus in priestly robes (plaster cast from the original).

Philosopher, Roman copy of Greek original.

Ammon, Roman (2nd century A.D.).

ROOM 2
(Giotto and the 13th century)

Above: **the Stygmata of St. Francis, School of B. Berlinghieri**; *below*: **Madonna and Child, Florentine School, 13th century.**

During the 13th century, Tuscan painters gradually broke away from the traditional modes and schemes of the Byzantine world. The process basically involved abandoning the hieratic rigidity of form and the representation of immutable, immobile eternal values: the new painters will paint more solidly and with less stiffness, they will attempt a closer adherence to reality and will try to represent man and his history. This transformation went ahead, one imperceptible step at a time, for about a century, but is to be appreciated and relished in all the Italian artists of the time, from the least known to the renowned Giotto, the real revolutionary of his century, in Italy.

St. Francis with the Stigmata, School of *Bonaventura Berlinghieri*, c. 1228.

Bonaventura, son of Berlinghiero, belonged to a family of painters who were chiefly active in the Pisa and Lucca areas. The Byzantine tradition in these territories was still very strong and is more evident in the central figures of the great altar-pieces, whereas the little figures in the surrounding scenes, and in the smaller panels are illustrated with greater narrative freedom and gusto.

Madonna and Child with Saints and Crucifixion, school of *Bonaventura Berlinghieri*, c. 1228.

The Redeemer with the Virgin, and Sts. Peter, John, and Paul, by *Meliore di Jacopo*, 1271.

The figures of Meliore's altar-piece blend traditional themes with the asperity, characteristic of the Coppo di Marcovaldo circle. The cherubims in the roundel were added in the 15th century.

16

Crucifixion and Episodes from the Passion, Tuscan School, 2nd half of the 12th century.

Above: **Madonna and Child enthroned, by Cimabue**; *below*: **the Redeemer with the Virgin, and Saints Peter, John and Paul, by Meliore di Jacopo.**

Crucifixion and Passion scenes, Tuscan school, 2nd half of the 12th century.

Madonna and Child enthroned, by *Cimabue*, c. 1280-1285.

The painting is also known as the *Madonna di Santa Trinita* as it was painted for the main altar of the church of Santa Trinita in Florence. Cenni di Pepo, better known as Cimabue, is universally recognized as one of the painters who changed the course of 13th century, and ultimately of all, Italian art. He is traditionally believed to have been Giotto's teacher. Even though his style is still, strictly speaking, Byzantine, new elements, such as an attempt to create spatial depth (note the superimposition of the figures and the freer-moving line), are readily evident. An attempt to depict three-dimensional space – a real break with the flat, abstract Byzantine spatial conception – is also noticeable in the curvature of the base of the throne behind the prophets. Although the figures are still hieratic they are fuller and the faces and gestures of the prophets are more expressive.

Madonna and Child enthroned, by *Giotto*, c. 1310.

Giotto was art history's great innovator, for it was Giotto who first spoke the new pictorial language that broke away from the rigid Byzantine tradition cleaving once more to Classical art. The best way to appreciate Giotto's innovations is to compare his enthroned Madonna with the other two versions of the same subject displayed in this hall. This, altarpiece painted c. 1310 for the church of Ognissanti in Florence shows him at the height of his artistic splendour. Although some traces of Byzantine influence still persist (for example, the gold ground and the stacking of the angels as if they were standing on a slope), the Virgin sits solidly in a credibly three-dimensional fashion and all the figures possess physically realistic space-encumbering bodies.

Badia Polyptych, by *Giotto*.

Also known as the Badia Altarpiece, this painting dates from the early 1300s.

Madonna and Child enthroned, by *Duccio di Buoninsegna*.

The Sienese master Duccio painted this altarpiece for the *Compagnia dei Laudesi*, a religious confraternity, in 1285. It is also known as the *Rucellai Madonna*, since for many years it hung in the Rucellai Chapel in the Church of Santa Maria Novella in Florence. Like Cimabue, Duccio is still tied to the Byzantine tradition, although in a different way. Here the throne, seen from a three quarters angle, is rendered with less solidity and the figures of the angels seem to float in the air against the gold ground. Instead of Cimabue's monumental figures, Duccio evokes a more intimate atmosphere in which the subtle interplay of line and colour is his main interest. This refined decorative tendency will characterize all Sienese 14th century painting.

St. Luke the Evangelist, by the *Magdalen Master*, 2nd half of the 13th century.

Crucifix with Stories of the Passion, School of Lucca, mid - 1200s.

Madonna and Child, Florentine school, mid - 1200s.

Above: **St. Luke the Evangelist, by the Master of the Magdalen;** *below*: **detail of the Badia Polyptych, by Giotto.**

Above, left: **Giotto's Madonna and Child enthroned**; *right*: **Duccio di Buoninsegna's**; *below*: **Badia Polyptych, by Giotto.**

ROOM 3
(14th century Sienese School)

During the «post Giottoesque» period, Florence and Siena developed the Gothic painting trend along diverging lines. The Florentines, remained basically true to Giotto's guidelines, whilst the Sienese tended to adopt Duccio as their lead. It was Duccio's reelaboration of the Byzantine tradition that inspired the elegant, airy draftsmanship of Simone Martini, with his transcendental, idealized beauty, so perfectly suited to the new «courtly» culture. Simone's long stays at the Papal court of Avignon and the Angevin court of Naples were to influence him profoundly, whereas Pietro and Ambrogio Lorenzetti attempted to blend the Sienese «post-Duccio» tradition with the Giottoesque innovations.

Presentation of Christ at the Temple, by *Ambrogio Lorenzetti*, c. 1342.

Ambrogio was the younger of the two Lorenzetti brothers and was more influenced by Giotto's new forms and contents. A cultured man of letters, as well as a painter, he was probably one of the first Italian artists to use his art to broadcast a political message, when he painted the *Allegory of Good and Bad Government* on the walls of the Hall of the Nine in the Palazzo Pubblico in Siena. His altarpiece in the Uffizi is the central section of a tryptych painted for the Cathedral of Siena and reveals his attention towards the problems of perspective. The building, in which he sets his scene, is shown both from the inside and from the outside according to traditional canons, but the depth of the space he manages to evoke is unprecedented for his time.

Scenes from the life of St. Nicholas of Bari, by *Ambrogio Lorenzetti*, c. 1330.

The four scenes represent: *St. Nicholas gives three poor girls their dowry; the Saint is elected Bishop of Mira; he resuscitates a boy strangled by a devil; he frees Mira from famine.* Some of the scenes manage to achieve a highly dramatic quality (specially the episode of the boy) and are both daring and evocative in character.

Presentation of Mary at the Temple, by *Niccolò Bonaccorsi*.

Active in Siena from 1372 to 1388. This panel was probably part of a tryptych and can be related to a panel in the National Gallery (London).

Nativity, by *Simone de' Crocifissi*.

Simone, an Aemilian painter, is still intensely influenced by Vitale da Bologna; his scenes are arranged with great compositional freedom.

Scenes from the life of the Blessed Humility by *Pietro Lorenzetti*, 1341.

The Lorenzetti brothers fused the Sienese decorative tradition with the new Florentine style introduced by Giotto. In this altarpiece, which shows the figure of the Blessed Humility in the centre flanked by eleven panels illustrating episodes from her life, Pietro offers a significant example of his lively narrative style in which naturalistic figures are placed in simple, yet clearly-defined, settings.

Left: Scenes from the life of St. Nicholas of Bari, by A. Lorenzetti; *above*: Annunciation, between Saints Ansano and Giulitta, by Simone Martini; *below*: Scenes from the life of the Blessed Humility, by P. Lorenzetti; *below, left*: two details from the same.

Sts. John, Mark, and Luke, by *Pietro Lorenzetti*, 1341.
These were originally the cusps from the Blessed Humility altarpiece.

Annunciation with Sts. Ansano and Giulitta, by *Simone Martini* and *Lippo Memmi*, 1333.

This triptych was painted for the Chapel of St. Ansano in the Cathedral of Siena. Simone Martini's typically Sienese approach is diametrically opposed to Giotto's. Whereas the Florentine master produces weighty, monumental figures, Simone creates refined, ethereal creatures out of sinuous curving lines and sets them against decorative gold grounds. This difference is especially noticeable in the treatment of the Virgin, whose graceful retiring pose contrasts greatly with the solemn immobility of Giotto's Madonnas. Simone, in fact, was both the initiator and leader of the school that dominated 14th century painting, known in art history as the International (or «flowery» Gothic) Style. Simone's brother-in-law, Lippo Memmi, painted the figures of the saints on either side.

Madonna and Child, by *Niccolò di Ser Sozzo Tegliacci*.

Niccolò, who together with Luca di Tommé, owned a flourishing Sienese workshop, was also, and chiefly, an illuminator of manuscripts: he was responsible for some of the greatest Italian illuminated codex masterpieces. He was a friend of Lippo Vanni and Lippo Memmi and together with them, followed in the footsteps of Pietro Lorenzetti. This Madonna was probably the central part of a tryptych and was stolen from the Church of Sant'Antonio in Bosco, near Poggibonsi in 1919. It was recovered and placed in the Uffizi in 1922.

Madonna and Child with Sts. Nicholas and Proculus, by *Ambrogio Lorenzetti*.

This tryptych, a magnificent example of Ambrogio's solid, elegant style, was painted in 1332 for the Florentine church of San Procolo (suppressed by Peter Leopold, Grand Duke of Tuscany). It stayed dismembered for centuries: the two side-panels were left for a long time in the Badia Fiorentina, whence they were taken to the Accademia and then to the Bandini Museum in Fiesole; the tryptych was finally reconstituted when the central panel was donated to the Uffizi by its owner, the art-critic Bernard Berenson, in 1959.

Virgin in Glory, by *Pietro Lorenzetti*.

This «Maestà» is one of the artist's earliest works (both Toesca and Berenson date it c. 1315); it is still visibly close to the Duccio di Buoninsegna mode, but also reveals the artist's painstaking familiarity with Giotto's innovations (Vasari significantly, albeit erroneously, says Giotto was his master), more apparent here, than in Pietro's later work. The Virgin's throne opens out in an attempt at perspective, similar to Giotto's (see the latter's enthroned Madonna in the preceding room), and the traditional lining of the drapery reveals solid, almost sculptural forms beneath the cloth, the infinite blue tonalities of which add further solidity to the whole. There is more: his youthful enthusiasm for new ideas and the extremely Gothic twist of the Mother's body as she turns to face her Child, which one only finds in Giovanni Pisano's sculpture.

Above: **Nativity, by Simone de' Crocefissi**; *below*: **Madonna and Child, by Niccolò di ser Sozzo Tegliacci**; *right*: **Presentation of Christ at the Temple, by A. Lorenzetti.**

ROOM 4
(14th century Florentine School)

Florentine 14th century painting could not avoid taking the extraordinary innovations of Giotto's teaching into account. The universality he had advocated was broken up into a series of related but individualistically limited experiences, that reflected the personalities of the innumerable pupils, followers and inheritors of the great master. Towards the middle of the century, an academic trend prevailed, which attempted to achieve technical perfection and paved the way towards the wider-spread European movement, called the International or «flowery» Gothic.

St. Cecilia and scenes from her life, by the *Master of St. Cecilia*, c. 1300.

One of the earliest and most devoted of Giotto's pupils. He followed the latter to Assisi and worked with him on the *St. Francis cycle* and expressed his master's teachings in his pleasant narrative style.

Madonna and Child enthroned, St. Francis with the Stigmata and two Saints, Crucifixion, by *Jacopo del Casentino*.

Madonna and Child, Angel, and Saints, by *Bernardo Daddi*.

Madonna and Child with Sts. Matthew and Nicholas, by *Bernardo Daddi*, 1328.

Crucifixion, by *Nardo di Cione*.

Below: **Crucifixion, by Nardo di Cione**

Virgin in Glory, by *Taddeo Gaddi*, 1355.

Taddeo Gaddi was, with Bernardo Daddi, the major representative of the Giottoesque school that flourished in Florence in the 14th century. Nevertheless, the Sienese influence, especially Ambrogio Lorenzetti's, may be felt in his work.

Deposition, by Tommaso di Sterano known as *Giottino*.

This painter, whom Vasari dubbed «little Giotto» is still shrouded in mystery, although his style is evidently a mixture of Lombard and Giottoesque influences.

Madonna and Child with Saints, by *Bernardo Daddi*.

This is a dismantled altarpiece. The subjects of the predella are seven episodes from the life of St. Anne, the Virgin, and a Nativity. There are also fourteen cusps with busts of Saints and Prophets.

St. Matthew and Scenes from his Life, by *Andrea Orcagna* and *Jacopo di Cione*, 1367.

Andrea Orcagna was the foremost Florentine painter of the 14th century. During this period the Giottoesque tradition, in which art was envisaged as a means of stressing and broadcasting the great moral and social issues of the age, was abandoned and the artists of Orcagna's circle focused their attention more on achieving technical perfection. This triptych is a typical example of Orcagna's refined approach.

Saints, Martyrs, and Virgins, by *Giovanni da Milano*.

Probably from the Ognissanti Altarpiece.

Above: St. Cecilia and scenes from her life, by the
Master of St. Cecilia; *below*: Madonna and Child with
Angels and Saints, by Bernardo Daddi.

Above: **Deposition, by Giottino;** *below*:
**St. Matthew and scenes from his life, by
A. Orcagna.**

ROOMS 5-6
(International Gothic Style)

Details from the predella of the Coronation of the Virgin, by L. Monaco.

Below: **detail of Thebaid, by G. Starnina.**

The evolution of the new International or «flowery» Gothic style was a European phenomenon, which involved artists of enormously different backgrounds and was applied to fields that ranged from painting, to architecture, to the lesser arts. The new attitude coincided with a widespread and refined admiration for beautiful things, which naturally led to a greater demand for all artistic products. Although the Church and, even more importantly, the Courts, continued to be the main inspirers and art patrons, the new wealthy classes, specially the merchant classes, started commissioning increasingly refined artefacts of precious materials and high technical perfection. The term «flowery» stresses the importance of the decorative element in this style, which is recognizable by its sinuous, entwining lines. There is a widespread and worldly interest in the present and its infinite variety; the idealistic teachings of history and Giotto's universality were abandoned and Simone Martini became the paradigm of the new courtly art.

St. Benedict blessing the poisoned wine, by an unknown Italian artist, 1st half of the 15th century.

Thebaid, by *Gherardo Starnina*.

The traditional attribution of this panel to Starnina has recently been questioned. In 1940, Longhi suggested that the painting might be the Angelico *Thebaid* mentioned in an ancient Medici inventory. Certain stylistic aspects have led other critics to date it is around 1420 at the earliest (Starnina died c. 1413). It certainly belongs to the Florentine school and painstaking attention to minute details in absolute typical 14th century «flowery» Gothic style make it a fascinating piece.

St. Benedict exorcising a Monk, by an unknown Northern Italian artist, 1st half of the 15th century.

Coronation of the Virgin, by *Lorenzo Monaco*, 1413.

Although the polyptych's frame has been heavily restored, its structure is in the complex Late Gothic style. It was painted in 1414 for the Florentine monastery of Santa Maria degli Angeli (today's Faculty of Letters), Lorenzo, a Camaldoli monk learnt his trade in Siena and Florence and was obviously much influenced by Simone Martini and his circle. His «flowery» style is still severely mystical and his still entirely Gothic rhythm and swirling lines are often (as in the Coronation) profoundly and densely tragic. The colour technique he has inherited from the old Sienese masters sometimes spreads out into brilliant expanses of colour and sometimes darkens, specially on the faces. Lorenzo's chiaroscuro, however, is not an attempt at suggesting depth, rather: an instrument of lyrical transformation. The severity of the darker visages counters the delicious, almost frivolous bubbling golden curls, the forest of cusps, turrets, twining columns, little shrines and multi-lobed panels. An altarpiece in Lorenzo's time was something that had to be put to practical use, and as such, the middle of the lower edge of the painting has unhesitatingly been cut away to make room for a shrine.

Above: **Coronation of the Virgin, by Lorenzo Monaco;** *below*: **Thebaid, by Gherardo Starnina.**

Four Saints, by *Gentile da Fabriano*, 1425.

The four panels with St. Mary Magdalen, St. Nicholas, St. John the Baptist and St. George belong to a polyptych that was broken up during the last century and divided up among four museums. The altarpiece had been painted for the church of San Niccolò sopr'Arno in Florence. The Royal Collection of Hampton Court (London) possesses the central part: a *Madonna and Child*; four scenes from the predella (with *Episodes from the life of St. Nicholas*) are in the Pinacoteca Vaticana (Rome); the fifth scene from the predella is in the National Gallery in Washington. Gentile was one of the most eminent representatives of the «flowery» style. He was born in the Marches and was schooled by Lombard masters (some of whom probably belonged to the Milanese manuscript illuminating circle). He spent his life in a continual search after new ideas and stimuli. At the beginning of the 15th century, we find him in Venice, where he worked on a fresco in the Doges' Palace (today lost) and passed on some of his ideas to Jacopo Bellini and Pisanello. Later, he moved on to Rome, Siena, Florence, Orvieto and then back to Rome, where he worked in San Giovanni in Laterano. Whilst in Florence, he became acquainted with Masolino and Masaccio, the teachings of whom he applied in a purely Gothic mode, which is apparent in the solemn Quaratesi Saints with their elegant, compact, fully solid forms and colours.

Adoration of the Magi, by *Gentile da Fabriano*.

Gentile painted this altarpiece for the Strozzi Chapel in the Santa Trinita church. It is the epitome of the International style, the profusion of gilding and extravagant costumes reflecting the refined taste of Palla Strozzi, the wealthy merchant who commissioned it. The artist's attention is focused on the cortège winding deep into the background. The fairytale figures and objects are represented in decorative flowing lines. No detail is deemed too unimportant to be left out. One can hardly believe that Gentile's fascinating storybook world belongs to the same years as Masaccio's simple stately universe.

St. Benedict mends his nurse's tray, by an unknown Northern Italian artist, 1st half of the 15th century.

Crucifixion, by *Agnolo Gaddi*.

Madonna and child with four Saints, by *Giovanni di Paolo*.

In the conservative atmosphere prevailing in Siena at the beginning of the 15th century, Giovanni di Paolo emerged as the representative of the most lyrical and fantastic trend, where the importance of the line triumphs over the relevance of form, in his pursuit of absolute, transcendental values.

Adoration of the Magi, by *Lorenzo Monaco*, c. 1420.

Compared with Gentile's Adoration, Lorenzo Monaco's seems rigorously ascetic, without the amused decorative additions in Gentile's crowded panel. This Camaldoli monk managed to add a touch of mystical contemplative simplicity to the elaborate, highly decorative International Style. Lorenzo's style is characterized by a pastel palette, akin to a miniaturist's and simple landscapes against gold grounds. This work was painted for the church of San Marco c. 1420.

Above and below: **Mary Magdalen, St. Nicholas, St. John the Baptist and St. George, from the Quaratesi Polyptych, by Gentile da Fabriano.**

Above and below: **Predella details from Magi Adoration, by G. da Fabriano.**

Adoration of the Magi, by Gentile da Fabriano; *below*: **Adoration of the Magi, by Lorenzo Monaco, with detail,** *left*.

ROOM 7
(Early 15th century Florentine school)

At the beginning of the 15th century, a new, organic conception involving mankind, the world and the artistic sphere developed in Florence. A revolution that was comparable to Giotto's innovations at the end of the 13th century, which managed however to affect the cultural evolution of the whole of Europe, by sparking off a vast, multi-faceted movement, which was later to be known as the Renaissance. Art, for the Humanists, is no longer a merely mechanical matter and becomes an intellectual activity. Artists take on new and freer rôles and are increasingly untrammelled by traditional ideological limitations. They learn to choose and defend their choice of style and content. Reality becomes the chief source of inspiration as regards the latter, although both themes and techniques vary widely. Reality and nature are subjected to study and research and art is the means mankind uses to research mankind, protagonist of history. In the course of this detailed investigation, the artist tries to rationalize reality as it appears to him. The most valid instruments for this rational approach are the laws of perspective, which oblige reality to conform to a unitary and coherent conception of the world. The first person to formulate these laws was an architect: Filippo Brunelleschi, and another architect, Leon Battista Alberti organized Brunelleschi's principles into a formal treatise on the subject. Humanism in sculpture was introduced by Donatello, whereas Masaccio led the way in painting. The great artists of the more advanced Renaissance era (Leonardo, Raphael and Michelangelo) owe an enormous debt to the courageous, fundamental innovations of these early «revolutionaries» of the 15th century.

Coronation of the Virgin, by Giovanni da Fiesole, known as *Fra Angelico*, c. 1430.

This panel comes from the church of Sant'Egidio; it reveals a number of typical features of Angelico's art: the seemingly unsophisticated arrangement of the scene, the brilliant transparency of the colours and the intense sweetness of the general atmosphere of the painting.

Madonna and Child, by Giovanni da Fiesole known as *Fra Angelico*.

Fra Angelico's painting is wholly devoted to religious and doctrinal themes. A Dominican friar, and one of the most involved in the life of the San Marco Monastery, Fra Angelico studied Masaccio. Although he appreciated and absorbed Masaccio's revolutionary innovations, he used them as tools for the expression of religious ideals. From Masaccio he learned to model lifelike rounded figures, yet he placed them in otherwordly settings, surrounded by the unreal light emanating from the traditional gold ground.

Madonna and Child enthroned with Sts. Francis, John the Baptist, Zenobius and Lucy, by *Domenico Veneziano*.

Known also as the Santa Lucia dei Magnoli Altarpiece, as it was painted for this Florentine church between 1445 and 1448. Domenico was influenced by Masaccio, but he was also susceptible to the charm of Gentile da Fabriano as well as being one of the first to appreciate the Flemish school

Above: **Madonna and Child with St. Anne, by Masolino and Masaccio;** *below*: **detail of the Madonna.**

Above: **Coronation of the Virgin, by Fra Angelico;** *below*: **Madonna and Child enthroned with Sts. Francis, John the Baptist, Zenobius and St. Lucy, by Domenico Veneziano.**

Above: **Madonna and Child, by Fra Angelico;** *below*: **Allegorical cart, by Piero della Francesca.**

innovations. He concentrated on the representation of light and space, which he managed to effect superbly in this painting, by piercing the depths of the loggia with an oblique shaft of sun-light slanting in over the right wall of the little court.

Madonna and Child with St. Anne, by *Masaccio* and *Masolino*, 1424.

Masaccio in painting, Brunelleschi in architecture, and Donatello in sculpture are the three key figures in Early Renaissance (first half of the 15th century) art. Masolino da Panicale, Masaccio's teacher, began this work by painting in the enveloping maternal figure of St. Anne. Masaccio's hand has been recognized in the figures of the Child and His Mother whose stately sculptural quality recalls Giotto rather than the courtly ladies of the International Style. Masaccio, like Giotto, expresses an inner, spiritual, beauty with his stately, almost architecturally plastic figures radiating strength and self-reliance.

Portraits of Battista Sforza and Federico da Montefeltro, by *Piero della Francesca*, c. 1465.

The two allegorical scenes on the back are symbolic references to the subjects portrayed on the rectos. In these portraits, painted at the court of Urbino, Piero reveals the influence of Flemish portraiture in both subject matter and style. The pitilessly and minutely effigied heads fill the foreground against a clear-cut, distant landscape, in true Flemish style. Piero's great importance lies in his acting as a link between the artistic tradition of Central Italy and the new trends developing in Northern Europe. He was especially interested in problems of perspective and, in fact, is the author of a treatise entitled *De Prospectiva Pingendi*. Piero arrived in Florence as a very young boy, in 1439, and worked with Domenico Veneziano in Sant'Egidio. Here he also took part in the avid dissertations on the laws of perspective, opting firmly for the positions of Paolo Uccello.

Portrait of Battista Sforza, by Piero della Francesca.

Battle of San Romano, by *Paolo Uccello*, c. 1456.

That Paolo Uccello had a fanatical passion for perspective is well known. In this painting, the foreshortened views of the horses, space-defining lances, and the patterning of simple geometric shapes against the sombre-coloured patchwork landscape, create a kind of unreal abstract composition. This abstractness in fact, lends Uccello's painting its special charm and «modern» quality. It is part of a set of three battle scenes (one is in the Louvre, and another in the National Gallery of London) commissioned by the Medici family and reputed to have hung in Lorenzo the Magnificent's bedroom in Palazzo Medici-Riccardi on today's Via Cavour. Paolo Uccello was probably the most eccentric among the early 15th century «revolutionaries». He was also the most discontinuous as regards stylistic coherence. This characteristic, as well as the lack of biographical details have made it extremely difficult to date and even attribute many of his works correctly. Among the most incontrovertible of his masterpieces are the frescoed *Scenes from the Genesis*, painted in the Cloisters of Santa Maria Novella and the delightful *Hunting Scene* in the Ashmolean Museum in Oxford.

Portrait of Federico da Montefeltro, by
Piero della Francesca.

Above: the Battle of San Romano, by Paolo Uccello; *below*:
detail of same.

ROOM 8
(Filippo Lippi)

Filippo Lippi (c. 1406-1469) is a central figure in the evolution of Florentine 15th century painting. He managed to tone down the violent disagreements that riddled Florence after the extremist attitudes taken by Paolo Uccello. Filippo followed in Masaccio's footsteps, accentuating the naturalistic aspects of the scenes and introducing a sentimental note that we fail to find, for instance, in Andrea del Castagno's or even in Masaccio's rigorous historical sense. From this point of view, he appears much akin to Luca della Robbia. The Flemish practice of crowding close up to the subject one was portraying or of filling the foreground with the subject, exercised a fundamental influence on Lippi. Among his most memorable works, not including the Uffizi paintings, one should recall his frescoes in the Cathedral of Prato, the Tarquinia Madonna *in the Galleria Nazionale (Rome) and the* Annunciation *in the Florentine church of San Lorenzo.*

St. Frediano deviates the Serchio River, Annunciation of the death of the Virgin, St. Augustine in his study, by *Filippo Lippi*, c. 1440.

Predella of the Barbadori Altarpiece in the Louvre.

Annunciation, by *Alessio Baldovinetti*.

Madonna and Child enthroned with Saints, by *Filippo Lippi*, c. 1455.

The altarpiece was originally in the Noviziato (Novitiate Chapel) in Santa Croce.

St. Francis receiving the Stigmata, Miracle of Sts. Cosmas and Damian, Nativity, Martyrdom of Sts. Cosmas and Damian, Miracle of St. Antony, by *Francesco Pesellino*.

Predella of the Madonna and Child enthroned with Saints altarpiece, by Filippo Lippi.

Madonna and Child with Saints, by *Alessio Baldovinetti*, 1453.

This altarpiece can be dated c. 1454, thanks to the manifest Andrea del Castagno characteristics it reveals; in 1454, in fact, Alessio Baldovinetti was working under Andrea on a painting of the *Last Judgement* (no longer extant) in the church of the Santissima Annunziata (Florence). The Uffizi altarpiece shows the *Virgin and Child surrounded by Saints Francis, Cosmas and Damian, John the Baptist, Laurence, Anthony Abbot and Peter the Martyr* and was commissioned by the Medici family for the chapel in the Cafaggiolo villa.

Coronation of the Virgin, by *Filippo Lippi*, 1447.

The panel was painted for the High Altar of the church of Sant'Ambrogio; it is an extraordinarily elegant composition, although it conforms to a traditional scheme. The saints standing opposite each other at each end of the painting are Sts. Ambrose and John the Baptist, whereas the two little kneeling friars (bottom left) are portraits of Lippi (with his hand under his chin) and his patron. The two roundels at the top, with the *Annunciation*, were added later.

Above: **detail of Coronation of the Virgin, by F. Lippi;** *below*: **detail of Novitiate Chapel altarpiece Madonna, by F. Lippi.**

Above: **Coronation of the Virgin, by Filippo Lippi;** *below*: **detail of the Madonna of the Adoration of the Child with Saints and the Madonna of the Novitiate Chapel, both by Filippo Lippi.**

Annunciation and Saints, by *Filippo Lippi*, c. 1450.

Triptych of the Resurrection of Lazarus, by *Nicolas Froment*.

The central panel of this magnificent tryptych, with its original frame, represents the *Resurrection of Lazarus*, while the side-panels show *Jesus meeting Martha* and *Mary Magdalen anointing Christ's feet*. When the side panels are closed over the central one, one side shows a *Madonna and Child*, whilst the other side shows *Francesco Coppini from Prato*, who commissioned the tryptych, kneeling in prayer. The latter was Papal Legate in Flanders and gave the tryptych to Cosimo the Old de' Medici. Cosimo donated the work to the Monastery of Bosco ai Frati in the Mugello area. Nicolas worked in the Provence between Avignon and Aix en Provence, where the most varied schools and influences met and blended together: Flemish, German and, strongest of all, the Italian School.

Madonna and Child with two Saints and two Angels, by *Matteo di Giovanni*.

Madonna and Child enthroned, with Saints, by Lorenzo di Pietro known as *Il Vecchietta*.

Madonna of the Rosary, by *Sandro Botticelli*.

Young Botticelli was apprenticed to two of the greatest Florentine artists of the early 15th century: Filippo Lippi between 1465 and 1467 and Verrocchio in the following two years, when the soft, lyrical, dreamy atmosphere which he had absorbed in Lippi's workshop was one of his most characteristic traits.

Third door (15th century) of the Uffizi Portico, restored after the 4th November 1966 flood.

Sinopia and Fresco of Nativity, by *Paolo Uccello*.

Madonna of the Loggia, by *Sandro Botticelli*.

Two miracles of St. Benedict, by *Bartolomeo di Giovanni*.

Adoration with St. Hilarion, by *Filippo Lippi*, c. 1465.

Madonna and Child with two Angels, by *Filippo Lippi*, c. 1465.

One of Lippi's late works, it is also one of his most renowned. Fra Filippo Lippi, a Carmelite monk, came under Masaccio's influence, but, although he profited from Masaccio's technical innovations, his approach was more intimate, more sensual that the great master's. The key to this work, which originally hung in the Medici villa at Poggio Imperiale, is his masterful use of soft colours which delicately model the forms and the shimmering light that gilds both the foreground figures and the airy landscape in the background.

Adoration of the Child with Sts. John and Romualdus, by *Filippo Lippi*.

This panel is thought to have been painted after 1463, for the Monastery of Camaldoli, which is why a monk of the Camaldoli order is represented kneeling in the lower right corner. He could be either St. Romualdus or St. Bernard.

Above: **Madonna of the Rosary, by Sandro Botticelli**; *below*: **detail of the Adoration with St. Hilarion, by Filippo Lippi**; *opposite*: **Madonna and Child with two angels, by Filippo Lippi.**

ROOM 9
(Pollaiolo)

The brothers Antonio and Piero del Pollaiolo were born in 1431 (Antonio) and c. 1443 (Piero). Their surname, as it usually did in Florence, at that time, indicated their father's occupation (poultry merchant). Conforming to another prevalent custom of the time, they were active in various artistic sectors: they were both sculptors, goldsmiths and painters. Antonio entered the world of art by learning the goldsmiths craft in the workshop of Vittorio Ghiberti, the son of the more famous Lorenzo, who had cast the Doors of Paradise *for the Baptistery (which Vasari states Antonio probably worked on too). He started painting fairly early and both activities were closely intertwined, leading him to work indifferently, either on a reliquary, on the design for a set of embroidered holy vestments or on the decoration of a tourney helm. His career ended in Rome, where he worked in the Vatican Grottoes. Piero, on the other hand, started out as a painter under Andrea del Castagno; his earliest production comprised the frescoes and the panel for the chapel of the Cardinal of Portugal in San Miniato al Monte in Florence. He later worked a lot with his brother.*

Six Virtues, by *Piero del Pollaiolo*.

Piero was commissioned a series of panels depicting the Virtues for the Council Chamber of the Merchant's Guild Hall in the summer of 1469. The first to be painted was the figure of Charity; the last was Fortitude, which was also one of the first works painted by Botticelli (1470). Piero del Pollaiolo's Virtues were used as models for the Virtues sculpted on the tomb of Pope Sixtus IV in the Vatican Grottoes, which he worked on together with his brother Antonio, between 1484 and 1493.

Fortitude, by *Sandro Botticelli*.

The Banquet of Queen Vasti, by *Jacopo del Sellaio*.

Hercules and the Hydra, by *Antonio del Pollaiolo*.

Hercules and Anteus, by *Antonio del Pollaiolo*.

These two tiny panel paintings were stolen in 1955 and only in 1963 were they recovered having turned up in the United States. They are oustanding examples of the distinctive style of Antonio del Pollaiolo, sculptor and goldsmith, as well as painter. The figures burst with a dramatic force achieved by means of tension expressed in line. The same tension is trasmitted to the surrounding landscape which is harsh and contorted. Its intense, vibrant luminous quality is totally unlike the clear radiance that bathes the landscapes of Piero della Francesca, Pollaiolo's contemporary. One of Antonio's fundamental tenets was a close adherence to the 15th century Florentine ideal of nature, which is expressed in his painstaking attention to the aspects of movement and his careful analysis of the human body and its anatomy. The *Martyrdom of St. Sebastian* at the National Gallery in London and the bronze statuette of *Hercules and Antaeus*, at the Bargello Museum in Florence follow the same guidelines. The dynamic quality of the latter, as well as the contorted expression on the faces of the protagonists manage somehow to express a satisfying, balanced harmony.

Faith
Justice

Temperance
Hope

Charity and Prudence, six Virtues by P. del Pollaiolo: *below*: Sts. Vincent, James and Eustace, by A. and P. del Pollaiolo.

The Return of Judith, by *Sandro Botticelli*.

The Discovery of the Corpse of Holophernes, by *Sandro Botticelli*.

This diptych, with the *Stories of Judith* was painted by Botticelli in his youth, and can be attributed to c. 1470, when Lippi's influence is still very noticeable, which is particularly evident in the way the figures (especially Judith's) relate to the landscape where the contours melt into a luminous vibrancy and the soft flutter of the drapery and wide splashes of colour recall Lippi's flowing grace. Judith's charm is in the gentle turn of her head and in the soft melancoly of her expression.

Portrait of a Lady, by *Antonio del Pollaiolo*.

This painting has been attributed to Antonio del Pollaiolo, although recent and less recent critics have assigned it to Piero della Francesca, Cosimo Rosselli and even Leonardo da Vinci. As there is absolutely no doubt that Antonio painted the *Portrait of a Lady* at the Poldi Pezzoli Museum in Milan, which strongly resembles the Uffizi one, it is highly unlikely that Piero della Francesca painted the latter. Piero's portraits are of the same matter and importance as his landscapes in the background and are part of them (see, for instance, the effigies of the Duke and Duchess of Urbino in Room 7). Antonio, on the other hand etches out his portraits against a neutral ground. All the light and colour in the painting together with the communicative potential, is concentrated into his subjects' faces and expressions.

Portrait of Youth with Red Hat, attrib. to *Filippino Lippi*.

Sts. Vincent, James, and Eustace, by *Antonio and Piero del Pollaiolo*.

The so-called Altarpiece of the Three Saints was painted c. 1467 for the Chapel of the Cardinal of Portugal in the church of San Miniato al Monte in Florence. The crest at the top of the beautiful original frame, is the cardinal's family crest. Vasari affirmed that the panel was jointly painted by both brothers, but the original documentation only mentions Piero. Most critics tend to exclude Antonio on the basis of stylistic considerations: the figures are in inconsistent relationship with each other as regards their size and the draftsmanship is somewhat naïve. The figures are compressed into an exigous space which evokes Piero's somewhat abrupt style. Notwithstanding or perhaps even because of its amost abstract or «primitive» traits, the painting is indisputably fascinating.

Portrait of Galeazzo Maria Sforza, by *Antonio and Piero del Pollaiolo*.

This portrait was, characteristically for the period, painted c. 1471, shortly after the visit payed to Florence by Galeazzo, Duke of Milan. He had succeded Francesco Sforza in 1466 and was stabbed to death by three assassins exactly ten years later. His son Gian Galeazzo inherited the ducal throne, but due to the fact that he was a minor, spent the early part of his life under the regency of his mother, Bona of Savoy first, and later of his uncle Ludovic the Moor.

Above: **Fortitude;** *below:* **detail of the Return of Judith, both by Sandro Botticelli.**

Above: Hercules and the Hydra, and Hercules kills Anteus, by Antonio del Pollaiolo; *below*: the Return of Judith and Discovery of the corpse of Holophernes both by Sandro Botticelli and Portrait of a Lady, by Antonio del Pollaiolo.

ROOMS 10-14
(Botticelli)

Alessandro Filipepi, called Botticelli, was no exception to the 15th century Florentine rule that made it easier for an artist to be born into a working-class family. The artistic profession was not considered sufficiently dignified for a member of the upper classes, although the first exceptions to this rule occurred in Florence itself, with Alberti and Brunelleschi. Mariano Filipepi, was a tanner, but he sent his son to learn the painter's craft in the workshop of Filippo Lippi. Three years were spent with the latter, then young Sandro moved to Verrocchio's workshop, where he spent a further two years, after which, in 1470, he set up shop on his own. A couple of years later, he became the master of Lippi's son, Filippino. Almost immediately, he attracted the patronage of the Magnificent Lorenzo (thanks to which, for instance, he managed to get the commission for a «Fortitude» – one of the Virtues – (which he «defrauded» Piero del Pollaiolo of) for the Council Chamber of the Merchants' Guild Hall. From then on, Sandro received more and more commissions: he worked for the great cemetery in Pisa, he painted the frescoed St. Augustine in the Ognissanti church in Florence and was given public commissions, such as when he was told to portray the hanged murderers who had taken part in the anti-Medici Pazzi Plot of 1478. He painted three frescoed scenes for the Sistine Chapel in Rome, but above all he worked for Lorenzo and for the other members of the Medici family. These were the years in which serried philosophical and literary debates took place at the Medici court, with Ficino, Pico della Mirandola and Poliziano spreading the recently re-discovered neo-Platonic doctrines. The classical world, with its myths and ideas was the object of reappraisal and quasi-veneration. Botticelli's part in this scenario is of fundamental importance. Around 1490, he underwent a sudden change of character. He was assailed by a religious crisis and was almost fanatically seduced by Savonarola's mystical reform. His style and attitude of mind underwent a radical change. The political crisis after Lorenzo's death, the expulsion of the Medici family from Florence and an accusation (that was never proven) of sodomy, changed Sandro's last years into a poverty-stricken purgatory, during which he only received a slender number of unimportant commissions. Botticelli's work probably represents one of the highest points of Florentine 15th century civilization: a heartrending and miraculous moment of equilibrium in which ideal beauty is given perfect expression. The recently restructured Botticelli room is crossed by three great wooden beams, from the dismantled theatre built by Buontalenti in the Uffizi for the Medici.

Above: **Portrait of an Unknown Man with a Medallion with Effigy of Cosimo the Elder;** *below*: **St. Augustine in his Study, both by Sandro Botticelli.**

Portrait of Unknown with Medallion with Effigy of Cosimo the Elder, by *Sandro Botticelli*.

Some believe this is a Botticelli self-portrait.

Adoration of the Magi, by *Filippino Lippi*.

Madonna and Child with Sts. John the Baptist, Victor, Bernard, and Zenobius, by *Filippino Lippi*, 1486.

The work is also known as the *Madonna degli Otto*.

Overall view of the new Botticelli Room; *below*: Madonna and Child enthroned with Angels and Saints; *and right*: Annunciation, both by Sandro Botticelli.

ROOMS 10-14 *continued*

Annunciation, by *Sandro Botticelli*.

Painted c. 1490 for the Cistercian church in Borgo Pinti in Florence, which used to be where the convent of Santa Maria Maddalena de' Pazzi stands today. The artist was deep in the throes of his religious crisis. It was in these years that he commenced illustrating Dante's Divine Comedy, for Lorenzo di Pierfrancesco de' Medici, adopting his fanatical, almost visionary later style.

Madonna and Child with Saints, by *Domenico Ghirlandaio*.

The altarpiece was painted (c. 1484) originally for the church of San Giusto alle Mura. St. Justus is in fact one of the saints standing around the Virgin together with St. Zenobius and the two archangels Michael and Raphael. This work, like most of Domenico Ghirlandaio's production shows the more «facile» side of Florentine painting in the 15th century, the uncomplicated, technically perfect, extraordinarily untrammelled, matter-of-fact attitude of certain successful painter-craftsmen.

St. Augustine in his Study, by *Sandro Botticelli*.

Madonna and Child enthroned with Saints, by *Sandro Botticelli*.

The so-called St. Barnabas Altarpiece, from the name of the church it was painted for, is dated c. 1487-89. In 1717 it was ruthlessly enlarged and repainted by Agostino Veracini, who also separated the main panel from the predella; in the 1930s the painting was restored to its original appearance. Botticelli was in the throes of his mystical, religious change of heart, when he gave up trying to return to the ideal balanced harmony of a mythical Golden Age and plunged into tormented spiritual research. The Apollo-like serenity of the earlier period is replaced by a more sombre atmosphere, a tauter line and, on the contents level, a kind of sense of guilt that leads the painter to forswear all his previous allegiances and adopt quasi - Gothic attitudes reminiscent of Angelico.

Predella of the St. Barnabas Altarpiece, by *Sandro Botticelli*.

Four scenes are shown: *Salome with the head of John the Baptist; Bishop St. Ignatius' heart is removed from his body, after his death; Christ after being taken off the Cross; St. Augustine and the Child on the sea-shore.*

Adoration of the Magi, by *Domenico Ghirlandaio*, 1487.

The artist was apprenticed to his father, a goldsmith, and worked for some time in his workshop, after which he followed Alessio Baldovinetti's work. He was also indirectly influenced by young Leonardo, Botticelli and Hugo van der Goes. Although he never took a very active part in the ideological discussions that were raging in Florence at the time, Ghirlandaio maintained his production at a very high qualitative level, which earned him both Raphael's and Vasari's esteem, to the extent, that the latter says that Ghirlandaio was one of the «best of his age». Domenico knows what his audience and patrons want and gives them his elegant draftsmanship, his shining spatial sense, brilliant colours and his tendency to be a chronicler of his era, introducing places and personalities of his time into his

Above: **Madonna and Child with Saints, by Filippino Lippi;** *below*: **Allegory, by the same.**

Above: **Adoration of the Magi**; *below*: **Madonna and Child with Saints, both by Domenico Ghirlandaio.**

St. Jerome, by Filippino Lippi.

Two details from the St. Barnabas Altarpiece predella, with Christ after being taken off the Cross and Salome with the Baptist's head, by Sandro Botticelli.

scenes. A large number of artists, specially his relatives, are trained in his workshop, one of the most famous being Michelangelo Buonarroti.

Saints lives, by *Domenico Ghirlandaio*.

The Predella, once in the church of Santa Maria a Monticelli, came to the Uffizi in 1919.

Venus, by *Lorenzo di Credi*.

Adoration of the Shepherds, by *Lorenzo di Credi*.

Lorenzo was apprenticed to Andrea del Verrocchio, alongside Leonardo da Vinci, whose way of handling light and space in landscapes influenced him considerably. He was later to be almost as deeply influenced by Perugino. When he was converted to Savonarola's ideas, at the end of the 15th century, he felt obliged to destroy all his un-religious works. The only painting of a pagan subject that has reached us is the *Venus* in this room, which was found during the last century in a cupboard in the Medici villa of Cafaggiolo. His *Adoration of the Shepherds*, dated c. 1510, comes from the church of Santa Chiara. It is characteristic of Lorenzo's last period, with its mystical and sentimental religious feeling.

St. Jerome, by *Filippino Lippi*.

This panel used to belong to the Badia Fiorentina, and is uncertainly attributed to c. 1480-1496. It is one of the best paintings by Sandro Botticelli's most renowned pupil. Filippino disregards the spiritual torment of his master and concentrates painstakingly on reality, which he then transposes into a fantastic dream-world. His attitude towards history and his time is that of a learned humanist researcher, rather than that of a mere chronicler; he is drawn to details, he is fascinated by meticulous portraiture and is always on the look-out for some aspect that will produce an unusual picture. The story of the painter's birth enables one to catch a glimpse of the relationship between art and public morality in the 15th century and is worth recounting: Filippo Lippi, the Chaplain friar of the Convent of Santa Margherita a Prato, was commissioned by the abbess to paint an altarpiece in 1456; he thereupon asked for permission to model the face of the Virgin on the beautiful face of one of the nuns in the convent: Lucrezia Buti. A few days later the two ran away together to Filippo's home. Shortly afterwards they were joined by Lucrezia's sister Spinetta, who was also a nun. Scandal ensued and the two nuns were forcibly taken back to their convent (by officers of the Law) where they were made to promise to «mend their ways». Hardly a year went past before they once more escaped from the convent and settled, this time for good, in Filippo's house. This time it was only thanks to Cosimo the Old's influence that the two lovers managed to evade the clutches of the Law. As Vasari recounts, Lucrezia gave Filippo «a son, who was christened Filippo as well and, like his father, was an excellent and famous painter».

Adoration of the Child, by *Filippino Lippi*.

Adoration of the Magi, by *Sandro Botticelli*, c. 1475.
Painted for the Lami Chape! in Santa Maria Novella and

Above: **Venus, by Lorenzo di Credi;** *below*: **Portrait of an old man, by Filippino Lippi.**

Above: the Calumny of Virtue, by Sandro Botticelli; *below*: Self-portrait, by Filippino Lippi and
Adoration of the Magi, by Sandro Botticelli.

extremely interesting from a historical viewpoint since it is filled with portraits of famous figures of the day, such as Botticelli himself (extreme right wearing a yellow cloak), Cosimo the Elder (the old man kneeling before the Virgin), Cosimo's son, Piero the Gouty (kneeling in the center with a red cloak), young Lorenzo the Magnificent (left foreground) and Giuliano, Lorenzo's brother (opposite side, darksuited figure).

Allegory of Spring, by *Sandro Bottricelli*, 1478.

One of Botticelli's most outstanding works painted at the height of his artistic maturity. Dated 1477-1478, it was commissioned by Lorenzo di Pierfrancesco de' Medici, Lorenzo the Magnificent's cousin. The title, Allegory of Sping, comes from the interpretation that Vasari gave to it, but its real meaning (it is full of references to neo-Platonic thought, the philosophic school which dominated Florentine culture in those years) has long been debated. It is now widely held that the subject was taken from «*Stanze per la Giostra di Giuliano de' Medici*» (Verses for the Joust of Giuliano de' Medici), by Agnolo Poliziano. The painting alludes to the «reign of Venus» – and the goddess is shown in the midst of a luxuriant garden of fruit and flowers. Starting from the left, the other figures are: Mercury, the three Graces in their revealing drapery, Flora strewing flowers, Chloris chased by the Zephyr wind, and winged, blind Cupid shooting his fateful arrows from above.

Calumny of Virtue, by *Sandro Botticelli*, c. 1495.

This is one of the artist's late works. It is full of symbolic meanings and Classical references, but it probably also refers to events in the lifetime of the artist perhaps to calumny directed against Botticelli himself or against Savonarola, of whom Botticelli, toward the end of his life, was a follower. The painting is an idealized reproduction of a very famous work, described in many Classical sources: the Calumny of Virtue that is supposed to have been painted by Apelles in antiquity. The naked figure of Truth, pointing at the sky, modelled on the «Venus pudica» (of which the Medici Venus in the Uffizi Tribuna is an excellent version) is particularly striking.

Madonna of the Pomegranate, by *Sandro Botticelli*, c. 1482.

The splendid carved and gilded frame, decorated with lilies, seems to indicate that the painting was commissioned by one of the offices in Palazzo della Signoria. The panel is one of Sandro's best traditionally handled religious paintings without philosophical undercurrents, which gained him much popularity. Botticelli's workshop was much in vogue up to the 1490s, after which it received very few commisions; the painter even offered his services to the Este court at Ferrara, but was refused by Isabella, duchess of Ferrara. It was at this point that the inexplicable unpopularity of an artist who up to a few years previously, had enjoyed the highest possible public esteem commenced: Leonardo criticised him for his insufficient precision as regards perspective, Vasari absent-mindedly praised the grace of some of his figures. At the end of the 18th century, his fame was totally obscured. It was

Above: detail from the Allegory of Spring; *below*: Pallas Athene and the Centaur, both by Sandro Botticelli.

Above: **Allegory of Spring;** *below*: **the Madonna of the Pomegranate and the Madonna of the Magnificat, three famous masterpieces by Sandro Botticelli.**

only with the English 19th century art-lovers that pre-Raphaelite interest in 15th century Florentine art and the an interest in Botticelli, who, at first, is chiefly appreciated for his vague melancoly and quasi-primitive naïveté re-awakened. It was not until the present century that the complexity of his intellect was fully appreciated.

Pallas Athene and the Centaur, by *Sandro Botticelli*, c. 1482.

Brought to the Uffizi in 1922, from Palazzo Medici. The picture is an allegory recalling Lorenzo the Magnificent's diplomatic success in Naples in 1480.

Birth of Venus, by *Sandro Botticelli*, c. 1486.

This painting too was commissioned by Lorenzo di Pierfrancesco de' Medici for his villa at Castello. Despite the fact that it was painted eight years after the Spring, it reveals the same melancholy, nostalgic spirit, the same delicately modelled figures, here culminating in the ethereal, naked Venus rising out of the sea, and the same wealth of symbolic meaning derived from neo-Platonic thought. Like the Spring, it was inspired by a poem of Poliziano's: Venus is born from the sea-foam and blown ashore by the seabreezes in a shell. On the right, her handmaiden welcomes her ashore, offering her a flowery cloak. Once more, as in the *Allegory of Spring*, Venus is at the centre of a complex, extraordinarily densely significant work. We might as well explain why this goddess of the pagan Olympus awakened so much interest. One of Botticelli's most important patrons, Lorenzo di Pierfrancesco, a cousin of the Magnifico, was introduced to the neo-Platonic philosophy and to the admiration of the Classical world by the main representatives of Florentine humanism, such as the poet Agnolo Poliziano and the philosopher Marsilio Ficino. Botticelli, as member of the Medici entourage was inevitably involved in this scenario and Lorenzo di Pierfrancesco became one of his main patrons. According to neo-Platonic thought, Man communicates with the Divine through Love; the central position of the erotic element underlies the central position of the Goddess of Love in all the mythological representations of the period. The Venus of the Allegory of Spring is the moderating influence in the season which embodies the most emphatic surge of vitality in the annual cycle. She acts as supreme harmonizer between impetuous blind Eros shooting his flaming arrows and the languor of the Three Graces (Chastity, Beauty and Voluptuousness) and the ardour with which Zephyr envelops Chloris in his sweet breath, transforming her into Flora, the generator of all flowers. The Venus of the *Birth* is, on the other (hand like the figure of Truth in the *Calumny of Truth*), a *Venus pudica* and the double nature of Love (chastity and sensuality) is wholly expressed in the simple gesture of the goddess, that unites the two aspects symbolizing the way humanity has to take in order to overcome its earthly confines to achieve the divine. Botticelli composed his picture as if it had been a melody or a poem which recalls Poliziano's melodious sweetness and evocative strength. Upon closer examination, however, the classical, harmonious symmetry of the picture is disrupted by indefinably dissonant elements such as Venus's "excessively" long neck, the oddly jointed left arm, the conventionally rendered waves, all of which are obscurely disquieting.

Above: **detail from Birth of Venus, by Sandro Botticelli;** *below and opposite, left*: **two Annunciation panels, from Hugo van der Goes' Portinari Tryptych.**

Above: the Birth of Venus, by Sandro Botticelli;
below: the Body of Christ being taken to the
Sepulchre, by Rogier van der Weyden.

Madonna of the Magnificat, by *Sandro Botticelli*, c. 1482.

This is one of Botticelli's greatest paintings on a religious theme. It is characterized by a warm-hued palette and rhythmically flowing line. The graceful composition is enhanced by the figures gathered around the Virgin and Child. The title of the painting comes from the first word appearing in the open book the Virgin is writing in.

Self-portrait, by *Filippino Lippi*.

Portrait of an old man, by *Filippino Lippi*.

Once in the Collection of Cardinal Leopoldo de' Medici.

Allegory, by *Filippino Lippi*.

Predella of the San Marco Altarpiece, by *Sandro Botticelli*.

Portinari Triptych, by *Hugo van der Goes*.

The huge altarpiece in the center of the hall represents the Adoration of the Shepherds. Van der Goes was commissioned to paint it in Bruges by Tommaso Portinari, the Medici's representative in Flanders. The triptych was sent to Florence in 1479 and placed in the Portinari's family chapel in the church of Sant'Egidio. The members of the sponsor's family are shown along with Sts. Thomas, Margaret, and Mary Magdalen. Van der Goes was one of the major representatives of the Flemish naturalistic School and this painting was to exercise enormous influence on all the late 15th century Florentine painters. Hugo van der Goes' life was saddened by a mental illness that constrained him to long years of inaction. In 1475, at the height of his career, he became a lay brother in a monastery affiliated to the confraternity of Windesheim. From then on, an irremediable breach between his sincere submission to the austere monastic rule and the worldly considerations to which he was continually exposed and invincibly attracted by, in the houses of his numerous noble patrons, ate into his soul. There is an echo of Hugo's religious beliefs in this composition: he was one of the first painters to introduce humble beggar-like figures in a religious scene, representing them (in accordance with the Windesheim precepts) on the same plane and with the same respect for their individual dignity as the other venerated figures in the *Adoration* scene.

The body of Christ taken to the Sepulchre, by *Rogier van der Weyden*, c. 1450.

Up to the last century, one was not even aware that Rogier van der Weyden had existed, and up to the middle of the present century, most of his works continued to be attributed to other masters. Many of his paintings, went on being assigned, for instance, to a hypothetical "Master of Flémalle", instead of being recognized as the youthful handiwork of Rogier. Intensive studies have finally managed to reconstruct this great Flemish master's life-work. He certainly trained as a miniaturist and was much influenced by Jan van Eyck in the early part of his career, although he adopted a harsher outline and colder colours. The Nicodemus supporting the body of the Christ and starting staight at the onlooker, is traditionally taken to be a self-portrait of the artist.

Above and below: **two details from the Portinari Tryptych, by Hugo van der Goes.**

Above: the Portinari Tryptych, by Hugo van der Goes; *below*: two details from the side-panels.

ROOM 15
(Leonardo da Vinci)

Room 15 is the first of the original grandducal gallery rooms; it contains works by Leonardo da Vinci and his circle. Leonardo was the perfect Renaissance Man: peerless artist, scientist, inventor, musician and man of letters; hungrily curious and tormented by an unquenchable thirst for knowledge. As Sigmund Freud wrote: "he was like a man who wakes up too early, in pitch darkness, while everybody else is still sleeping". He was born in Vinci in 1452 as illegitimate son to Piero d'Antonio and a woman of the place, named Caterina. In 1469, his family moved to Florence and he was apprenticed to Verrocchio. After working with his master on various projects, he was commissioned work on his own account: a panel for Palazzo Vecchio and the Adoration of the Magi. In 1482 he went to Milan to work at the court of Ludovic the Moor. There he worked as civil engineer, as builder of war machines, he painted the Virgin of the Rocks and the Last Supper for the Refectory of the Santa Maria delle Grazie Monastery. In the following years, he was constantly on the move between Florence, Milan and Rome, until, in 1517, he finally accepted the invitation of the king of France, François I, his great admirer and entered his service permanently. On the 2nd May 1519, Leonardo died and was buried in Amboise, in the church of Saint Florentin. A few years later, during the Wars of Religion, his remains were dispersed.

Allegory of Fruitfulness, by *Luca Signorelli*.

Three predella panels, by *Luca Signorelli*.

Crucifixion with Mary Magdalen , by *Luca Signorelli*.

Below: **detail from the Deposition from the Cross, from the Crucifixion with Mary Magdalen, by Luca Signorelli.**

Annunciation, by *Leonardo da Vinci*.

One of his earliest paintings, it was painted in 1470, when Leonardo was still apprenticed to Andrea del Verrocchio, for the Monastery of Monteoliveto in Florence. The attribution has been hotly debated and a number of art historians feel that it should be attributed to Ghirlandaio. Uncertainty derives mainly from the somewhat cold, schematic treatment of the scene, so totally lacking in the *sfumato* technique typical of Leonardo. Yet the delicate, fluid treatment of the figures, the accurate description of detail, and the skilfully handled landscape fading into the distance to corroborate the attribution to young Leonardo da Vinci seem.

Immaculate Conception and six Saints, by *Pietro di Cosimo*.

Baptism of the Christ, by *Andrea del Verrocchio* and *Leonardo da Vinci*.

Leonardo as a very young apprentice, gave proof-here of his remarkable artistic maturity; the angel on the left, as well as the landscape in the background, are both supposed to be his.

Adoration of the Magi, by *Leonardo da Vinci*.

Leonardo served his apprenticeship in Andrea del Verrocchio's workshop in Florence, and it was the Florentine artistic tradition which underlay his unique stature as an artist. His genius explored many fields including science, architecture,

Above: **Annunciation, youthful work by Leonardo da Vinci;** *below, left*: **Crucifixion with Mary Magdalen, by Luca Signorelli;** *right*: **detail from the background of Leonardo's Annunciation, where his masterly «sfumato» technique causes the landscape to dissolve into the distance.**

music, engineering, townplanning and literature. Painting, to Leonardo, was no longer just a representation of reality, but a tool of scientific research, the intellect's arm for penetrating the secrets of the laws of nature. This Adoration, which Leonardo left unfinished when he moved to Milan in 1482, already shows the artist at the height of his artistic maturity. By means of his special *sfumato* technique, he dissolves contour outlines, and, by placing his figures in a new dynamic way, frees the composition from rigidly codified tradition.

The Three Archangels and Tobias, by *Francesco Botticini and Andrea del Verrocchio.*

Annunciation, by *Lorenzo di Credi.*

Perseus frees Andromeda, by *Piero di Cosimo.*

The Trinity, Madonna and Child, Angels and Saints, by *Luca Signorelli.*

Lament over the Dead Christ, by *Pietro Perugino.*

Predella of the Trinity, by *Luca Signorelli.*

Above: **Annunciation, by Lorenzo di Credi;** *below*: **two Angels, from Baptism of Christ, by Verrocchio and Leonardo da Vinci.**

ROOM 16
(Map Room)

The room takes its name from the territorial maps of Tuscany painted in oil pigments on the walls by Ludovico Buti and Stefano Buonsignori. The maps represent the "ancient Florentine domains", the territories of the State of Siena and of the Isle of Elba *and were painted by order of Ferdinand I de' Medici. Nine canvases depicting mythological subjects have been set into the ceiling and were commissioned from Jacopo Zucchi by Ferdinando de' Medici while he was in Rome, and was still in cardinal. The canvases represent:* Diana and the nymphs; Night; Pan; Endymion asleep; Mercury, Faithfulness; Patience; Silence *and* Vigilance.

ROOM 17
(of the Hermaphrodite)

The room used to contain mathematical instruments and cosmological maps, hence the ceiling grotesques, depicting scientific instruments. The central position is occupied by Mathematics. *They were painted between the 16th and 17th centuries, possibly by Giulio Parigi. For reasons of security, the gate is kept closed but can be opened upon request.*

Eros and Psyche, Hellenistic (2nd century B.C.).

The Sleeping Hermaphrodite, Hellenistic (2nd cent. B.C.) The room is full of statuettes, bronzes, and antique or Renaissance portrait busts.

Above: **Adoration of the Magi, by Leonardo da Vinci;** *below*:
Baptism of Christ, by Verrocchio and Leonardo da Vinci; *right*:
Immaculate Conception and six Saints, by Piero di Cosimo.

ROOM 18
(Tribuna)

The so called Tribuna was built for Francesco I de' Medici by Buontalenti. The elaborate decoration of the octagonal room topped by an imposing eight-sided dome completely lined with seashells, perfectly epitomizes 16th century Mannerist taste. The room was recently rearranged and restored as much as possible to its original appearance. In addition to an extraordinary collection of 16th century Mannerist paintings, there is an equally unique one of well-known Classical statues.

Octagonal Table, by *Jacopo Ligozzi*.

The octagonal shape of this table, placed in its original position, at the centre of the Tribuna, echoes the octagonal form of the room. The exquisite top in inlaid semi-precious stones, cut into the shapes of animals, flowers and decorative motifs was produced by the workshop of Jacopo Antelli, upon designs by Jacopo Ligozzi, except for the central roundel, which was designed by Bernardino Poccetti and Baccio del Bianco. The whole proves the high degree of technical and artistic perfection achieved by the Florentine craftsmen of the 16th and 17th centuries.

SCULPTURE:

Young Apollo, Greek, end of the 4th century B.C.

Its prototype is Praxiteles' Lyceum Apollo.

Scythian preparing to flay Marsyas, school of Pergamon, 3rd-2nd century B.C.

The statue is sometimes called the *Knife-grinder* since the figure is shown sharpening a knife.

Medici Venus, attributed to *Cleomenes,* middle of the 1st century B.C.

This superb example of Classical sculpture is a copy of the original by Praxiteles dating from the 4th century B.C. It was discovered in 1660 in Hadrian's Villa at Tivoli and brought to the Uffizi in 1717 by Cosimo III de' Medici.

Wrestlers, Greek, c. 2nd century B.C.

Dancing Faun, Greek, 3rd century B.C.

The statue is a Greek copy of an original by Praxiteles. The subject is really a satyr beating out the rhythm of a dance on a musical instrument known as a *"scabellum"*. The statue has undergone extensive restoration.

PAINTINGS:

Allegory of the Immaculate Conception, by *Giorgio Vasari.*

Portrait of Cosimo I, by *Agnolo Bronzino*, c. 1545.

Agnolo Allori, known as Bronzino, was appointed official painter to the Court of Cosimo I in 1539, following a period of joint collaboration with another famous Mannerist painter, Pontormo. Several of his court portraits are displayed here. These official portraits reveal the painter's typically detached, intellectual style: smooth gleaming forms. The most striking,

Above: **Medici Venus, Ist century B.C.;** *below*: **Scythian preparing to flay Marsyas, 3rd/2nd century B.C.**

Above: **overall view of the Tribuna;** *below*: **the Wrestlers, 2nd century B.C.**

ROOM 18 *continued*

in addition to Cosimo I, are Eleanor of Toledo, Lucrezia Panciatichi, and Maria de' Medici as a child.

Portrait of unknown woman, by *Andrea del Sarto*, c. 1514.

Original sin, by Carletto Caliari, known as *Carlo da Verona*.

Portrait of Eleanor of Toledo and her son, by *Agnolo Bronzino*.

This is one of the most beautiful portraits ever painted by Bronzino, who here gives proof of extremely high technical prowess. The key-note of the painting, that manages to triumph over the splendid melancholy visage of Eleonora, the daughter of the Viceroy of Naples and wife to Cosimo I de' Medici, is her magnificent brocaded and embroidered ceremonial gown. The virtuoso play of dazzling light caught in the stiff folds causes the gown to stand-out brillantly against the dead blue background. The child next to Eleonora is said to be the future Cardinal Giovanni de' Medici.

Portrait of unknown man dressed in black, by *Agnolo Bronzino*.

The Prophet Elisha, by *Giorgio Vasari*.

Portrait of a little girl, by *Agnolo Bronzino*.

Cherub playing a lute, by *Rosso Fiorentino*.

Vasari writes that Rosso Fiorentino was, at the height of his fame, involved in a distressing trial, brought upon him by slanderous accusations which grieved him to such an extent, that he decided to poison himself. If the words of this eclectic, Florentine artist and historian are to be believed, notwithstanding the sceptical attitude of many critics, Rosso's would appear to be the first known case of an artist's suicide. Giovan Battista di Jacopo de' Rossi, known as Rosso, was born in Florence in 1495 and continued to work in his native town until 1523. Later, we find him in Rome, in Umbria and in Venice and finally, in France, where François I entrusts him with the decoration of one of the halls in his castle of Fontainebleau. During his Florentine period, he painted some of his most beautiful works, in which the influence of both Andrea del Sarto and Pontormo is vividly apparent. They are frank, lively, typically "local" blends of cultured and popular tradition. The pretty little *Angel Musician* in the Tribuna was in fact painted in Florence, although one is not quite certain as to the dating of it, some preferring 1514-15, others 1522.

Portrait of don Garcia de' Medici as a child, by *Agnolo Bronzino*.

Madonna and Child, by *Giulio Romano*.

Creation of Eve, by Carletto Caliari, known as *Carlo da Verona*.

St. John in the desert, by *Raphael*.

Madonna of the Well, by Francesco Cristofano known as *Franciabigio*.

Leda and the swan, by *Jacopo Pontormo*.

Portrait of Francesco I de' Medici, by *Agnolo Bronzino*.

Above: **detail of the splendid dome of the Tribuna, decorated with sea-shells and mother of pearl;** *below*: **St. John the Baptist as a boy, in the desert, by Raphael.**

Above: **Portrait of girl with book**; *below*:
**Portrait of Lucrezia Panciatichi, both by
Agnolo Bronzino.**

Above: **Portrait of Don Garcia de' Medici,
as a baby**; *below*: **Eleonora of Toledo with
her son, both by Agnolo Bronzino.**

Portrait of Maria de' Medici, by *Agnolo Bronzino*.

Christ bearing the Cross, by *Cecchino Salviati*.

Portrait of Bartolomeo Panciatichi, by *Agnolo Bronzino*.

The Family of Adam, by Carletto Caliari or *C. da Verona*.

Charity, by *Cecchino Salviati*.

Portrait of Lucrezia Panciatichi, by *Agnolo Bronzino*.

Pale Lucrezia, with her gleaming alabaster complexion, looks at us out of this enth proof of Bronzino's ability as a portrait-painter. Daughter to Gismondo Pucci, she was married in 1528 to Bartolomeo Panciatichi, who was, for a brief period, Florentine ambassador to Lyons. The chain around her neck is engraved with the motto "Sans fin l'amour dure" (Love lasts without end) which was probably a memento of the couple's stay in France. The son of Bartolomeo and Lucrezia Panciatichi, Carlo who was gentleman-in-waiting to the Grand Duke Francesco I de' Medici, still had the portraits of his parents in his possession in 1584. At the beginning of the 18th century, the two paintings already belonged to the Grand Duke's collection.

Portrait of a gentleman, by *Ridolfo del Ghirlandaio*.

Portrait of a girl with a book, by *Agnolo Bronzino*.

Expulsion from Paradise, by *Jacopo Pontormo*.

Charity, by *Jacopo Pontormo*.

Portrait of Cosimo the Elder, by *Jacopo Pontormo*.

Expulsion from Paradise, by Carletto Caliari known as *Carlo da Verona*.

The painting, which is an agreable variation on the Biblical theme, that has been handled as if it were a mythological subject, is a youthful work of the Veronese painter. The series it belongs to also includes *Adam's Family*, the *Creation of Eve*, and the *Original Sin*, that are in the Tribuna too. They used to hang in a room of the Medici villa of Artimino.

Massacre of the Innocents, by *Daniele Ricciarelli da Volterra*.

Painted for the cathedral of Volterra, it was bought for the Uffizi in 1782 by Peter Leopold of Hapsburg-Lorraine.

Portrait of Lorenzo the Magnificent, by *Giorgio Vasari*.

Annunciation, by *Giovanni Bizzelli*.

Portrait of Bianca Cappello, by *Alessandro Allori*.

Once in the church of Santa Maria ad Olmi, in the Mugello area, this tempera came to the Uffizi in 1948. The passionate Venetian lover and later second wife to Francesco I de' Medici, with her brilliant, Titian-red hair, is portrayed in her sumptuously bejewelled court gown, posing for a formal portrait. The unfortunate lady suffered the enmity of her brother-in-law Ferdinand (Francesco's successor), who caused her body to be buried in an unknown tomb, forbidding his brother's body to be laid alongside his beloved Bianca's.

Above: **Octagonal table; by Jacopo Ligozzi;** *below*: **detail from the Massacre of the Innocents, by Daniele da Volterra.**

Above: **Cupid playing a lute, by Rosso Fiorentino;** *below, from left to right*: **Cosimo the Old, by Jacopo Pontormo; Daughter of Cosimo de' Medici, by Agnolo Bronzino; Lorenzo the Magnificent, by Giorgio Vasari.**

ROOM 19
(Signorelli and Perugino)

Pietro Perugino is the most important Umbrian master at the end of the 15th century; he was trained in austere Piero della Francesca's workshop, and acquired a more sophisticated touch in Florence, in Verrocchio's workshop, where he met and consorted with Leonardo. In due course, he became Raphael's master. Piero is also the foundation upon which Luca Signorelli (of Cortona) based his art, as well as being influenced by Pollaiolo's harsher lines. Luca's most famous works were the frescoes *with episodes from the* Last Judgement, *painted in the Cathedral of Orvieto.*

Madonna and Child with Sts. John the Baptist and Sebastian, by *Pietro Perugino*, 1493.

Pietro Vannucci known as Perugino, is one of the foremost Umbrian painters of the 15th century. His artistic formation was influenced to a great extent by Piero della Francesca and Verrocchio, as well as by Luca Signorelli, and his contemporary, Leonardo. Nevertheless, his clear, uncomplicated, and at the same time, almost mystical art was far removed from the complicated ideological debate which was then raging among the Florentine artists, led by Leonardo and Botticelli. This work, like many others by Perugino, is the result of the artist's attempt to achieve the most balanced and harmonious composition possible. The scene is set in the peaceful twilight preferred by the painter.

St. Sebastian, by *Lorenzo Costa*, c. 1492.

The Virgin Annunciate, by *Melozzo da Forlì*.

Martyrdom of St. Sebastian, by *Gerolamo Genga*.

The Annunciating Angel Gabriel, by *Merlozzo da Forlì*.

Portrait of a youth, by *Pietro Perugino* or *Lorenzo Costa*.

Crucifixion, by *Marco Palmezzano*.

Portrait of Evangelista Scappi, by *Francesco Francia*.

Pietà, by *Lorenzo da San Severino*.

Portrait of Francesco delle Opere, by *Pietro Perugino*, 1494.

Madonna and Child, by *Luca Signorelli*.

Portraits of Don Biagio Milanesi and Baldassarre, a Vallombrosan monk, by *Pietro Perugino*.

Holy Family, by *Luca Signorelli*.

The two works by Luca Signorelli displayed here are typical of the master's production. Signorelli broke away from the frozen, emotionless clarity of his teacher, Piero della Francesca, giving vent to his more dramatic and excitable personality (this feeling for the dramatic will be fully realized in Signorelli's turbulent Last Judgement frescoes in the Cathedral of Orvieto). The arrangement of the figures is in harmony with the shape of the tondo, which is the forerunner of Michelangelo's celebrated *Doni Tondo*, in Room 25.

Above and top opposite left: **the Annunciation, by Melozzo da Forlì**; *below*: **detail from the Holy Family, by Luca Signorelli.**

Above: **Madonna and Child with Sts. John the Baptist and Sebastian, by Pietro Perugino;** *below, left*: **Madonna and Child;** *right*: **Holy Family, both by Luca Signorelli.**

ROOM 20
(Dürer and the German School)

Albrecht Dürer, the greatest German Renaissance artist, a writer of treatises, painter and above-all engraver, was born in Nuremberg, on the 21st May 1471. His letters and diaries afford excellent and illuminating insights into his life. He received his first artistic training in the workshop of his father, a goldsmith, who was the first person he portrayed (portrait in this room). When he was fifteen, he was apprenticed to the Flemish painter Wolgemut. In 1490 he started on his travels all over Europe, coming into contact with a wide variety of styles and schools. He returned to Germany four years later, brimming over with newly acquired learning and experiences, and married Agnes Frey, the daughter of a rich merchant and left almost immediately afterwards for Italy. In Venice, he met Bellini and Carpaccio; in Padua, Mantegna, and copied the works that he was most struck by of all three. He continued his wanderings through Central Italy and in 1496 returned to Nuremberg, where he opened his own workshop. Years of great activity ensued, during which he concentrated chiefly on portrait painting and engraving. His 15 wood-cuts of the Apocalypse *are simultaneously the apex of the great German engraving tradition and the expression of Albrecht's passionate act of allegiance to the precepts of the Lutheran Reform. A lucid attachment to reality, painstaking attention to detail, an elegant, refined line are salient aspects of Dürer's art. He had by now become extremely famous and was much esteemed by the Hapsburg Emperors Maximilian I and Charles V. In 1515, he went to the Netherlands, where he met Metsys, Lucas van Leyden, van Orley and saw what the great 15th century Flemish masters had painted. He died in Nuremberg in 1528, of malaria which he had probably contracted in a Dutch swamp into which he had ventured in order to see a shark or whale that had been trapped in some fishing-nets.*

Adam and Eve, by *Lucas Cranach*, 1528.

Lucas Cranach, both painter and engraver, differs from his illustrious contemporary and fellow German Dürer, in that he retained more of the Gothic tradition and typical German expressionism in his style. A comparison of Cranach's Adam and Eve with Hans Baldung Grien's version of Dürer Adam and Eve hanging in this room reveals greater elongation of the figures which, in Cranach, exude a kind of tremulous sensuality. Cranach, a personal friend of Martin Luther, painted several portraits of the great theologian, one of which together with the one of his wife Catherine Bore, displayed here, are outstanding instances.

The Great Calvary, by *Albrecht Dürer*, 1505.

The Great Calvary, by *Jan Breugel the Elder*.
Copy from the Dürer.

St. James the Apostle, by *Albrecht Dürer*, 1516.

Eight episodes from the lives of Sts. Peter and Paul, by *Hans von Kulmbach*, c. 1509.
Sections of an altarpiece.

Adam and Eve (*opposite, top left*), **once in the Pitti Palace, they were moved to the Uffizi in 1922. They are copies of the Dürer originals in the Prado in Madrid, painted by Hans Baldung Grien, one of Dürer's best followers.**

Below: **Portrait of Catherine Bore, by Lucas Cranach the Elder.**

Above: **Adam and Eve, by Lucas Cranach;** *below*: **St. James (left) and St. Philip** (*right*), **by Albrecht Dürer.**

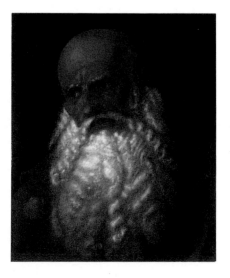

St. Philip the Apostle, by *Albrecht Dürer*, 1516.

Adam and Eve.
Copied by Hans Baldung Grien from the Dürer originals displayed in the Prado in Madrid.

Adoration of the Magi, by *Albrecht Dürer*, 1504.

Albrecht Dürer, trained as an engraver under the well-known master Martin Schongauer, although he soon revealed his great skill as a painter. His frequent travels around Europe kept him in touch with all the major artistic movements of his day and this wide-ranging artistic background produced a style which is a complex blend of the various European artistic traditions, especially Venetian. Dürer, in turn, greatly influenced 16th century Italian painting. In this superb Adoration of the Magi, he combines Flemish naturalism with a typical Venetian (especialy Bellini-like) feeling for modelled form and rich colours.

Portrait of the artist's father, by *Albrecht Dürer*, 1490.

One of Dürer's youthful works, this portrait, dated 1490, was painted before the artist was exposed to Italian Renaissance influences. In fact, it is in the style of a typical Flemish portrait. Together with the portrait of his mother, the painter painted this one of his father, so that he would have his parents' likenesses with him on his travels. Portrait painting (together with engraving) were the fields Dürer was most fascinated by during his maturity. His exploration and reconstruction of reality as a single organism, in which he analyses each separate element appear to find best expression in his portraits: when he analysed the physical aspect of his subjects he also seemingly attempted to express their thoughts and spiritual make-up. As from 1494-96, after his second trip abroad, Dürer adopted certain Italian techniques in his portrait painting, softening his contours and drawing on his Venetian experiences, with especial reference to Bellini.

Madonna and Child of the Pear, by *Albrecht Dürer*, 1526.

Portrait of unknown man, by *Joos Van Cleve*.

Portrait of Ferdinand of Hapsburg, by *Hans Maler*, 1524.

Portraits of John I and Frederick II of Saxony, workshop of *Lucas Cranach*.

Portraits of Martin Luther and Melanchton, by *Lucas Cranach*.

Portrait of a man, by *Hans Burgkmair*.

St. George, by *Lucas Cranach*.

Portrait of a lady, school of *Lucas Cranach*.

Self-portrait, by *Lucas Cranach*, 1550.

Crucifixion, German school of the 16th century.

Portraits of Martin Luther and his wife Catherine Bore, by *Lucas Cranach*.

Above: **Portrait of John I of Saxony**; *below*: **Frederick III of Saxony, School of Lucas Cranach the Elder.**

Above: **Adoration of the Magi, by Albrecht Dürer;** *below, from left to right*: **Madonna of the Pear, by Albrecht Dürer; Portraits of Martin Luther and Melanchton, by Lucas Cranach.**

ROOM 21
(Giovanni Bellini and Giorgione)

Towards the end of the 15th century and at the beginning of the 16th, a new kind of Renaissance style of painting emerged in the Veneto, in which colour and light predominated over the rigorous line that prevailed in Central Italian painting. The leaders of this movement were Giovanni Bellini and his youngest pupil, Giorgione.

Halberdiers and old men, by *Vittorio Carpaccio*.

Portrait of Giovanni il Bentivoglio, by *Lorenzo Costa*.

St. Ludovic of Toulouse, by *Bartolomeo Vivarini*.

Christ in the Temple at Jerusalem, by *Giovanni Mansueti*, mid-15th century.

Madonna and Child, by *Cima da Conegliano*.

Portrait of a gentleman, by *Giovanni Bellini*.

St. Dominic, by *Cosmè Tura*.

Sacred Allegory, by *Giovanni Bellini (called Giambellino* in Italian), the foremost artist of a whole family of painters who laid the foundations of 16th century Venetian painting. Giovanni trained under his father, Jacopo, a well-known painter in his own right, but was most influenced by his brother-in-law, Andrea Mantegna. In his painting, Bellini established a relationship of homogeneity between figures and landscape which are linked by the intense warm light modulating the tonal relationship between the colours. The atmosphere is serene and silent, the landscape is complex and harmonious. Despite the effort of countless art historians over the years, the subject of the painting has never been fully understood. One theory is that it is a *Sacra Conversazione*, although not all the figures have been identified, nor do we known the relationships between them. Other scholars, on the other hand, feel it is an allegory of Purgatory or even Paradise, while still others feel that the subject derives from a 14th century French poem entitled «*Le pélérinage de l'âme*» (Pilgrimage of the Soul). The work came into the Uffizi collection in 1793, thanks to an exchange with the Imperial Galleries of Vienna.

Lamentation of Christ, by *Giovanni Bellini*.

Judgment of Solomon, by *Giorgione* and others.

Man in armour with a squire, attributed to *Giorgione*. The subject is also known as the *Gattamelata*.

The Infant Moses being tried by fire before Pharoah, by *Giorgione* and others.

These three works have been attributed to Giorgione, to whom questionable attributions have often been made, only to be later withdrawn. He is almost certainly responsible for the clearly-defined landscapes fading into the distance, dominating the two Biblical scenes. Giorgione, together with Bellini, played a key role in the development of Venetian painting and was instrumental in the formation of Titian.

Above: **St. Ludovic of Toulouse, by Bartolomeo Vivarini;** *below*: **St. Dominic, by Cosmé Tura.**

Above: Holy Allegory, by Giovanni Bellini; *below left*: the Judgement of Solomon, attr. to Giorgione and Madonna and Child, by Cima da Conegliano (*right*).

ROOM 22
(Holbein and Altdorfer)

In Northern Europe, at the beginning of the 16th century, the tempestuous blast of the Reformation swept an almost insurmountable problem into many artists' laps: the most rigid protestants declared themselves adamantly against all forms of religious painting, inasmuch as it was interpreted as an idolatrous Papist tradition. It was in this climate that Hans Holbein the Younger's great art came into being and flourished. Hans was born in 1497, in Aachen, into a family of famous painters and engravers. As a youthful and precocious apprentice in the workshop of Hans Herbst in Basle, he came into contact with the Italian masters. In his thirties, he was already one the most esteemed German painters, but the Calvinist explosion forced him to look for work elsewhere and a letter written by Erasmus of Rotterdam reccomended his services to the English court of Henry VIII, where he concentrated on portrait painting. He died in London in 1543. His contemporary, Albrecht Altdorfer, had the curious habit of painting landscapes – even when the subject in hand had absolutely no open-air connotations – into his religious scenes or into any of his other paintings allowing vegetation to invade the whole scene. Altdorfer suffers the consequences of the Reformation too and due to the lack of commissions spends his last years as a practicing architect and town councillor in his home town of Regensburg.

Christ with the Crown of Thorns, by *Lucas van Leyden*.

Dutch painter and engraver, his works reveal painstaking psychological research. Influenced by Dürer, whom he knew personally, he later followed the custom of the times and studied the Italian masters, achieving an unmistakable «Roman» style in his later work. His drawings and numerous engravings (which are, at times, very large) are generally considered of greater interest than his paintings (as yet not very well known).

Portrait of unknown eighteen year-old, by *Georg Pencz*.

German painter and engraver, for a long time influenced by Dürer's style and technique. Later, in Italy, he studied Raphael's painting with enormous enthusiasm. His contemporaries greatly admired his usually small engravings and portraits.

Portraits of P. Baroncelli and his wife, by the *Master of the Baroncelli Portraits*.

Portrait of Benedetto di Tommaso Portinari, by *Hans Memling*.

Hans Memling, a German of Seligenstadt, lived and grew up in Bruges, in Flanders, where he had a workshop and achieved considerable fame. He became well-known abroad, receiving commissions from Spain, England and Italy, specially from Florence, which had had excellent trade dealings with Bruges for centuries. This portrait bears witness to this profitable state of affairs: the subject is Tommaso Portinari's son had commissioned the Portinari Tryptych from Hugo Van der Goes ten years earlier. The present panel is also part of a triptych, together with the *St. Benedict* in the same room and

Above: **Hans Holbein the Younger's Portrait of Sir Richard Southwell;** *below:* **Christ with the Crown of Thorns, by Lucas van Leyden.**

Above: **Departure and Martyrdom of St. Florian, both by Albrecht Altdorfer;** *below from left to right*: **Portrait of Sir Thomas More, by Hans Holbein the Younger; Portraits of an unknown man and his wife, by Joos van Cleve the Elder.**

a *Madonna and Child* in the Staatliche Museum in Berlin. The subject's mild absorbed expression, the painstaking craftsmanship, together with the soft, dreamy landscape make this one of the best portraits the artist ever painted.

St. Benedict, by *Hans Memling*.

Portrait of Unknown, by *Hans Memling*.

Portrait of a man, with landscape, by *Hans Memling*.

Madonna and Child enthroned with two Angels, by *Hans Memling*.

Portrait of Thomas More (?), school of *Holbein*.

Departure of St. Florian, by *Albrecht Altdorfer*, c. 1525.

Martyrdom of St. Florian, by *Albrecht Altdorfer*.

Probably son of the painter Ulrich, Albrecht achieved an early success thanks to his dramatic fairy-tale-like expressive qualities. He assigned an increasingly important rôle to both architecture and landscape, sometimes even allowing them to invade the whole scene, whereas most other painters of his time confined these elements to the background.

Self-portrait, by *Hans Holbein the Younger*.

Son to Hans the Elder, he was his father's pupil and one of the most important portrait-painters of his time. His first large paintings reveal perspective solutions and decorative motifs clearly derived from the Lombard school. He was to work for a long time in Switzerland and later at the court and for the aristocracy in England, where he instilled a measured equilibrium into his style, that he had absorbed from his acquaintance with Renaissance art.

Portrait of Sir Richard Southwell, by *Hans Holbein the Younger*.

Even though he was born a German, Holbein lived and worked primarily in England where he was court painter to Henry VIII. Like Bronzino at the Medici court, Holbein's official position led to a predominance of portraits in his oeuvre. This is an outstanding example of his skill in portrait-painting.

Portrait of an unknown man and his wife, by *Joos van Cleve the Elder*.

Deposition from the Cross, by *Gérard David*.

Portrait of an unknown man and his wife, by *Bernard van Orley*.

Mater dolorosa, by *Joos van Cleve*.

Crucifixion, by the *Master of the Virgo inter Virgines*, 16th century.

Adoration of the Magi, by *Gérard David*.

Madonna and Child with Sts. Catherine of Alexandria and Barbara, by the *Hoogstraeten Master*.

Above: **detail of landscape in Madonna and Child enthroned by Hans Memling**; *below*: **Mater Dolorosa by Joos van Cleve.**

Above: **Madonna and Child enthroned with Angels, by Hans Memling;** *below*: **Selfportrait, by Hans Holbein the Younger.**

Above: **Portrait of Benedetto di Tommaso Portinari, by Hans Memling;** *below*: **Madonna and Child with Saints, by the Hoogstraeten Master.**

ROOM 23
(Correggio and Mantegna)

It was not only in Rome, Florence or Venice that the greatest Italian Renaissance innovations occur. It was in the Aemilian province of Parma that the artistic activity of Antonio Allegri, known as Correggio, emerged. Correggio was the name of his native village. He was influenced at first by the late Classical style of Mantegna, but was not impervious to Leonardo's and Michelangelo's new ideas. Correggio draws upon antiquity for his repertory of beautiful forms and as a source of solutions for representing facts and personalities of his own time. In his religious paintings, he adopts a simpler, more direct language, in his search after effect and evocative images. He was the first to adopt a later much imitated way of decorating the San Giovanni Evangelista church and the Cathedral of Parma domes: he «pierces» through the domes to achieve a trompe l'oeil heavenly vision, which will be imitated by countless other painters for centuries to come.

Christ carrying the Cross, by *Giovanni Francesco Maineri*.

Portrait of a man, by *Bernardino dei Conti*.

The Executioner presents John the Baptist's head to Herodias, by *Bernardino Luini*.

St. Catherine of Alexandria, by *Giampietrino*, 1st half of the 16th century.

Portrait of Cardinal Carlo de' Medici (?), by *Andrea Mantegna*.

Adoration of the Magi, Circumcision of Christ, Ascension, by *Andrea Mantegna*, c. 1489.

Above: detail from the Ascension; *below*: Portrait of Cardinal Carlo de' Medici (?), both by Andrea Mantegna.

The triptych, painted for the Chapel of the Ducal Palace in Mantua, is variously assigned to c. 1464 and c. 1470. Andrea Mantegna, a Venetian from Isola di Carturo (1431-1506), spent his apprenticeship between Venice and Padua, where he was influenced by Jacopo Bellini and Vivarini, as well as by Andrea del Castagno and by the sculpture of Donatello. He immediately became familiar with the links between Classical myths and Christian iconology and the history/nature diatribes. The first and most important of his works were the *frescoes* in the Ovetari Chapel in Padua and the *San Zeno triptych* in Verona. In 1453 he married a sister of Giovanni Bellini. The Duke of Mantua's court presided over by the art-loving Gonzaga family took him on as court painter in 1460 and it is there he produced his mature works and exploited his considerable culture as Curator of the Ducal Collections. He painted his masterpiece on the walls of the Wedding-night Room (*Camera degli Sposi*), which is a complex fresco, framed by a complicated trompe l'oeil architectural arrangement and includes mythological figures and a rendering of two important episodes in the life of Francesco Gonzaga. He continued to be fascinated by the Classical world and allegorical subjects that he depicted with refined elegance, although his deeply tragic religious feelings were revealed from time to time in other work, like the beautiful and terrible *Dead Christ* in Brera (Milan).

Above: detail of the Adoration of the Magi and Madonna of the Quarries, by Andrea Mantegna;
below: Rest on the flight to Egypt and Adoration of the Child, both by Correggio.

Madonna of the Quarries, by *Andrea Mantegna*, c. 1489.

Portrait of Barbara Pallavicino, by *Alessandro Araldi*.

Portrait of a man, by *Giovanni Ambrogio de Predis*.

Christ amidst his tormentors, by Giovanni Antonio Bazzi known as *Sodoma*.

Sodoma, from Vercelli, travelled extensively in the first half of the 16th century, until he settled in Siena. He built up his flowing decorative style drawing on two great masters: Perugino and Leonardo. His painterly qualities have been somewhat re-appraised recently after having been much esteemed. He certainly enjoyed great fame in his lifetime and was even knighted by Pope Leo X, notwithstanding the reputation of a Sodomite he was credited with and which earned him the nickname he is still most known by. Vasari informs us that he was a «merry, licentious man and took great pleasure in living "dishonestly", wherefore, inasmuch as he was ever surrounded by striplings and beardless youths, whom he loved beyond all measure, he was called Sodoma; the which he was by no means offended by but gloried in». Vasari adds that Sodoma kept all manner of beasts in his workshop: apes, dogs, horses, asses, crows and jays.

Gypsy girl, by *Boccaccio Boccaccino*.

Narcissus at the spring, by *Giovanni Antonio Boltraffio*.

Madonna and Child, by *Vincenzo Foppa*.

Portrait of Guidobaldo da Montefeltro, attributed to *Raphael*.

Portrait of Elisabetta Gonzaga, attributed to *Raphael*.

Virgin in Glory, by *Correggio*.

Rest on the flight to Egypt, by *Correggio*.

Antonio Allegri was called Correggio after the name of his birthplace, a town in Northern Italy. His artistic training took place in the circle of Aemilian painters heavily influenced by Mantegna and Leonardo. This early work reveals the traits that characterize his whole production: balanced, harmonious composition based on diagonals in space and the counterpositioning of bright colours that glow in an intimate cozy setting shrouded in shadow.

Adoration of the Child, by *Correggio*.

ROOM 24
(Miniature Collection)

The gemstone collection (now in the Silver Museum in Palazzo Pitti) was once displayed in this room, designed by Zanobi del Rosso in the 18th century. The miniatures exhibited, both Italian and non-Italian, date from the 15th to the 18th centuries.

Above: **Portrait of Elisabetta Gonzaga;** *below*: **Portrait of Guidobaldo da Montefeltro, two splendid works attributed to Raphael. Both come from the Ducal Palace of Urbino and have been in the Uffizi for the past fifty years.**

Above: **Narcissus at the spring, by Giovanni Antonio Boltraffio:** *below*: **Portrait of Barbara Pallavicino, by Alessandro Araldi and Christ amidst his tormentors, by Sodoma.**

Above: **View along the second corridor;** *below*: **Boy removing a thorn from his foot, Roman copy, 2nd/1st century B.C.**

THE SECOND CORRIDOR

A short corridor joins the Uffizi's two main wings. The views from the windows on either side are superb. From the left side starting at the left, you see the hills surrounding Florence, in the distance, with the sparkling white façade of San Miniato on the hilltop, Forte Belvedere, and, in the foreground, the Arno River, crossed on the far right, by Ponte Vecchio. From the right side, you get a splendid view of the *Piazzale degli Uffizi* with Palazzo Vecchio towering majestically beyond it. The first stretch of the corridor contains lovely 17th century pergola-design ceiling frescoes. Like the first corridor, it is filled with superb Classical sculptures. The highlights are a *round Sacrificial Altar* (altar), with bas-reliefs showing the sacrifice of Iphigenia (neo-Attic, 1st century B.C.), the *Boy removing a thorn from his foot* (2nd-1st century B.C. Roman copy of a Greek bronze) *Crouching Venus* (copy of a Greek original by Doidalsas, 3rd century B.C.) the extraordinary *Seated girl preparing herself for the dance* (copy of a 3rd century B.C. Hellenistic original), and two seated *Roman matrons*.

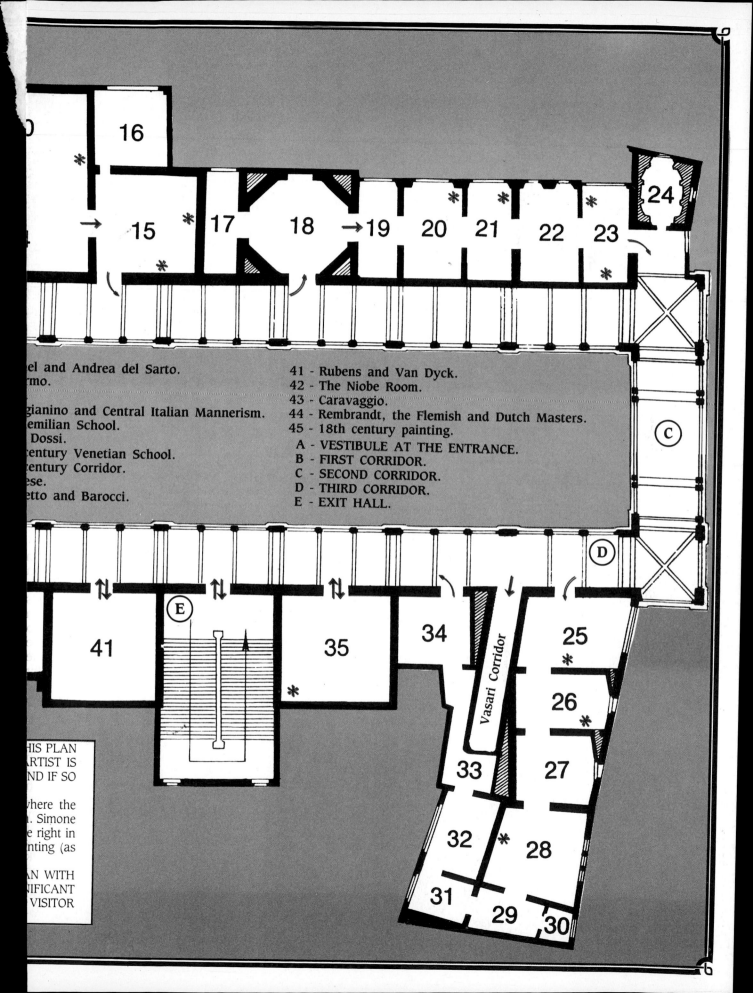

16

15 →

17

18 → 19

20

21

22

23

24

...el and Andrea del Sarto.
...rmo.

...gianino and Central Italian Mannerism.
...emilian School.
... Dossi.
...century Venetian School.
...century Corridor.
...ese.
...etto and Barocci.

41 - Rubens and Van Dyck.
42 - The Niobe Room.
43 - Caravaggio.
44 - Rembrandt, the Flemish and Dutch Masters.
45 - 18th century painting.
 A - VESTIBULE AT THE ENTRANCE.
 B - FIRST CORRIDOR.
 C - SECOND CORRIDOR.
 D - THIRD CORRIDOR.
 E - EXIT HALL.

C

D

E

41

35

34

25

26

Vasari Corridor

33

27

32

28

31

29

30

...HIS PLAN
...ARTIST IS
...ND IF SO

...here the
... Simone
... right in
...nting (as

...AN WITH
...NIFICANT
... VISITOR

THE UFFIZI GALLERY

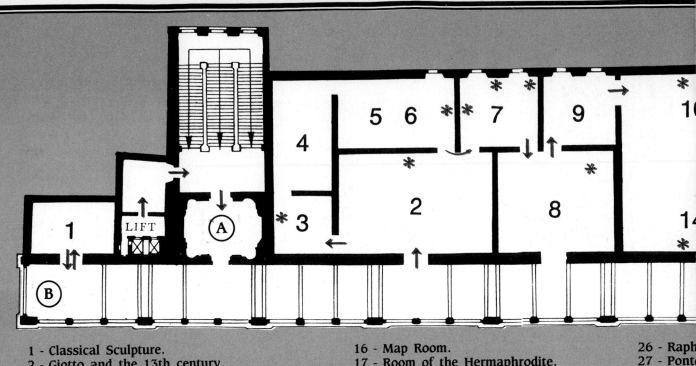

1 - Classical Sculpture.
2 - Giotto and the 13th century.
3 - 14th century Sienese School.
4 - 14th century Florentine School.
5/6 - International Gothic Style.
7 - Early 15th century Florentine School.
8 - Filippo Lippi.
9 - Pollaiolo.
10/14 - Botticelli.
15 - Leonardo da Vinci.

16 - Map Room.
17 - Room of the Hermaphrodite.
18 - The «Tribuna».
19 - Signorelli and Perugino.
20 - Dürer and the German School.
21 - Giovanni Bellini and Giorgione.
22 - Holbein and Altdorfer.
23 - Correggio and Mantegna.
24 - Miniature Collection.
25 - Michelangelo.

26 - Raph
27 - Ponto
28 - Titia
29 - Parm
30 - The
31 - Doss
32 - 16th
33 - 16th
34 - Vero
35 - Tinto

THE GENERAL INDEX OF THE ARTISTS ON PAGE 134 AND
ENABLE ONE TO FIND OUT IMMEDIATELY WHETHER A
REPRESENTED BY ONE OR MORE WORKS IN THE GALLERY
WHERE THE WORK/S IS / ARE.
For instance, after Simone Martini, the Index lists page 2
seventh description relative to Room 3 refers to his Annuncia
Martini is therefore represented by the seventh painting from
Room 3 which is in effect devoted to 14th century Sienese
the plan shows).
THE WORKS ILLUSTRATED LEFT AND MARKED ON THE
AN ASTERISK CAN BE CONSIDERED SOME OF THE MOST S
WORKS IN THE GALLERY WHICH EVEN A VERY HURR
SHOULD TRY NOT TO MISS (ONE/TWO HOURS).

ROOM 8
Madonna and Child,
by Filippo Lippi.

ROOMS 10-14
Birth of Venus,
by Sandro Botticelli.

ROOM 20
...tion of the Magi,
...Albrecht Dürer.

ROOM 21
Holy Allegory, by
Giovanni Bellini.

...d Francis

ROOM 43
Young Bacchus,
by Caravaggio.

ROOM 44
Self-portrait,
by Rembrandt van Rijn.

BELVEDERE TERRACE

ROOM 2
Enthroned Madonna
and Child, by Giotto

ROOM 3
Annunciation, by
Simone Martini.

ROOMS 5-6
Adoration of the Magi,
by Gentile da Fabriano.

ROOMS 10-14
Allegory of Spring,
by Sandro Botticelli.

ROOMS 10-14
Portinari Tryptych, by
Hugo van der Goes.

ROOM 23
Adoration of the Magi,
by Andrea Mantegna.

ROOM 23
Adoration of the Child,
by Correggio

ROOM 25
Holy Family (Doni Tondo
by Michelangelo Buonarr

ROOM 7
Federico da Montefeltro,
by Piero della Francesca.

ROOM 7
Battle of San Romano,
by Paolo Uccello.

ROOM 7
Madonna and Child,
by Masolino and Masaccio.

ROOM 15
Annunciation, by
Leonardo da Vinci.

ROOM 15
Adoration of the Magi,
by Leonardo da Vinci.

Ad

ROOM 26
Madonna of the Goldfinch,
by Raphael.

ROOM 28
Venus of Urbino,
by Titian.

ROOM
Sts. John the Baptis
by El Gr

Above: **detail of the ceiling in the second corridor;** *below*: **Girl preparing herself for the dance, 3rd century B.C. and Crouching Venus, 3rd century B.C.**

Ponte Vecchio (the Old Bridge), the river Arno and the hills seen through the windows of the second corridor.

THE THIRD CORRIDOR

At the beginning, on either side: statues of *Marsyas*, copies of 3rd century B.C. Hellenistic originals (the one on the right was restored in the 15th century by Donatello by order of Cosimo the Elder). Classical sculptures are displayed on both sides of the long corridor. Of particular interest a copy of Myron's *Discus-thrower, Leda and the swan* (Roman copy of a 4th century B.C. Greek original), *Dionysus and a young satyr* (Roman copy of a 4th century B.C. Greek original), another *Leda and the swan* (this one copied from Thimotheos), the *Citharist Apollo* (replica from the Hellenistic-Roman period), and, at the end, the *Laocöon*, Baccio Bandinelli's 16th century copy of the Hellenistic original in the Vatican Museum. On the left are the entrance to the *Corridoio Vasariano*, the vestibule leading to the museum exit, and, at the far end, the exit to the terrace on top of the Loggia della Signoria. The terrace affords a splendid view of Piazza della Signoria and was used for some time as

Above: the third corridor; *below* **Marsyas hung before his flaying, copy of a 3rd cent. B.C. Hellenistic original; Antinous, Roman art** (second corridor); **Laocoön, 16th cent. copy by Baccio Bandinelli.**

the private pleasure garden of Eleonora of Toledo, wife to Cosimo I de' Medici.

THE VASARI CORRIDOR

The entrance is in the third corridor between Rooms 25 and 34. The corridor, crossing the Arno via the Ponte Vecchio and connecting the Uffizi and Palazzo Vecchio to Palazzo Pitti, was commissioned by Grand Duke Cosimo I de' Medici. Vasari put it up in record time, five months in all, in 1565. During World War II it was badly damaged and was only re-opened to the public in 1973. The corridor is about half a mile long. All along it on either side the windows offer lovely views of the city, the river, and Ponte Vecchio itself. After crossing the Arno, the corridor goes through the church of Santa Felicita and standing in the newly-reopened balcony inside the church one looks down into the interior of the church through the gilded grille behind which the Grand Dukes of Tuscany once attended Mass. The Vasari Corridor is hung with paintings from the Uffizi's 16th and 17th century collection. The first rooms contain paintings by followers of Caravaggio, including *The Successful venture*, the *Banquet in Olympus* and *Banquet with luteplayer*, by Gerard van Honthorst; paintings by Rutilio Manetti; *Painting and architecture* by Francesco Rustici; *Judith and Holophernes*, by Artemisia Gentileschi and works by Guido Reni. Next come 17th century Italians, from Annibale Carracci to Guercino with his *Sleeping Endymion*. 17th century Italian schools, arranged according to geographical area are shown in the long corridor, the highlights of which are a *Sacra Conversazione* by Giovan Battista Crespi, the *Samian Sibyl*, by Guercino, a *Portrait of Cardinal Agucchia* by Domenichino, and works of the Neopolitan school from Salvator Rosa to Battistello Caracciolo, Cerquozzi, and Giuseppe Recco. See also the *Fair at Poggio a Caiano* by Giuseppe Maria Crespi, *Cupids in flight* by Giovan Battista Tiepolo, and, lastly, paintings by Rosalba Carriera and Pompeo Batoni. The most famous part of the *Vasari Corridor* is the section dedicated to self-portraits by Italian and non-Italian artists of every period. The Italians include Leonardo; Vasari; Agnolo Taddeo, and Gaddo Gaddi; Romanino; Andrea del Sarto; Bronzino; Titian; Jacopo Bassano; Palma the Younger; Veronese. The last section of the *Corridor* contains a collection of portraits of famous people of all periods.

Opposite: **Staircase leading down to the Vasari Corridor from the Uffizi;** *Above*: **the Corridor with the Self-portraits Collection;** *below, from left to right*: **Self-portraits of G.L. Bernini, Leonardo da Vinci and Diego Velasquez.**

Above: **Self-portrait, by Giorgio Vasari;**
below: **Self-portrait, by Antonio Canova.**

Above: **Self-portrait, by Rembrandt van Rijn;**
below: **Self-portrait, by P.P. Rubens.**

Above: **Interior of the church of Santa Felicita, seen through an opening in the Vasari Corridor;** *below, from left to right*: **Self-portraits of Eugène Delacroix, Jacques-Louis David and Angelica Kauffmann.**

ROOM 25
(Michelangelo)

Michelangelo Buonarroti, who was considerered the greatest artist of all time, while he was still alive, was born in Caprese, in Tuscany, on the 6th March 1475, into an ancient Florentine family. He was educated and trained in Florence in close contact with the newly formed neo-Platonic philosophical circle at the Magnificent Lorenzo's court. He subsequently fell under the spell of Savonarola's fiery sermons and later still declared his allegiance to the reformed Catholic precepts that he became acquainted with during his long, profoundly significant friendship with Vittoria Colonna, a noble Roman lady. These were the ingredients that provided the moral «stiffening» that transpires so overpoweringly from his works. It is sufficient to think of the David, *which was both a passionate declaration of republican ideals (inherited from his father) and a supreme model of virtue. Painter, sculptor and architect, he transformed European art for two whole centuries. He was dubbed «divine» by some and attacked by others for the harshness of his style and for the «untamed wildness» of his character. He was apprenticed to Ghirlandaio at thirteen, but did not get on very well with his master and after about a year started attending the Medici garden of San Marco, where he was initiated into the art of sculpture. His extraordinary career gave him the most important commissions of his time: his never completed* Battle Scene *for Palazzo Vecchio, but above all, the magnificent frescoes in the Sistine Chapel in the Vatican, commissioned by Pope Julius II. The immense task was accomplished by the artist, single-handed in barely four years. The result is generally considered to be the greatest masterpiece of all time. In the Vatican he built his architectural chez d'oeuvre: the dome of St. Peter's. Michelangelo ended his long life in Rome in 1564. His remains were later transferred, in accordance with his wishes, to Santa Croce in Florence.*

Visitation, by *Mariotto Albertinelli*.

Annunciation, Nativity, and Presentation at the Temple, by *Mariotto Albertinelli*.

This is the predella of the *Visitation*.

Apparition of the Virgin to St. Bernard, by *Fra Bartolommeo*.

Portrait of P. Perugino, attributed to *Raphael*.

Portrait of a lady, by *Giuliano Bugiardini*.

Holy Family, by *Michelangelo Buonarroti*.

This is one of Michelangelo's rare panel paintings. It is often referred to as the Doni Tondo, after the name of the patrons who commissioned it in 1504. The treatment of the figures clearly shows Michelangelo's propensity for sculpture, to which painting, according to the great master, was supposed to be adapted – the complete opposite of Leonardo's conception. The figures are animated by a dynamic tension which accentuates the heroic, monumental handling of the subject. The foreground group, the Holy Family, symbolizing the new realm of Christianity, is drastically separated from

Above: **detail from Doni Tondo** (*opposite*); *below*: **Portrait of P. Perugino, attrib. to Raphael.**

Above: the world-famous Doni Tondo, by Michelangelo; *below*: Annunciation, Nativity and Presentation at the Temple, by Mariotto Albertinelli.

the world inhabited by the line of nude youths in the background, symbolizing the Classical pagan world.

Moses defending the daughters of Jethro by *Rosso Fiorentino*.

Giovanni Battista di Jacopo, known as Rosso Fiorentino is, along with Pontormo, one of the key figures of the 16th century movement called Mannerism. The term was first used by Landi at the end of the 17th century, to disparagingly indicate a pictorial «manner» in vogue in the 16th century. The 17th century (and post-17th century) critics judged the style a cold, intellectual emulation of the great Renaissance masters (Michelangelo, primarily, but also Raphael and Leonardo). For a long time Mannerism was viewed as an unnatural exercise in pure virtuosity; it was not until the 20th century that it was re-evaluated as the dramatic expression of a tormented and contradictory historical period. In this painting which typifies Rosso's mature style, the dynamic tension and powerful rendering of the bodies reveal the strong influence of Michelangelo.

Christ before Caiaphas, by Francesco Ubertini known as *Bachiacca*.

Like many other Florentine artists of the time, Bachiacca was basically involved in repetitive, routine, decorative work, which, however, he carried out with impeccable style. The numerous commissions he received from his rich bourgeois clientèle were his reward. Researchers believe that this kind of work was chiefly inspired by the Northern Schools, that Bachiacca seemed to be well acquainted with. This painting clearly recalls a Dürer print of similar content. Michelangelo's influence is also noticeable.

Salome, by *Alonso Berruguete*.

Son to Pedro, a painter, Alonso owes his fame chiefly to his sculpture and architecture. His most significant works, drenched in mannerist feeling and already containing a foretaste of the Baroque, are in Spain. He was active in Italy, where he met Michelangelo, Leonardo da Vinci and Vasari. The Salome used to be attributed to Federico Barocci, but in the 1950s, Longhi traced it to Berruguete.

Joseph presents his father and brother to Pharoah, by *Francesco Granacci*.

At the beginning of the 16th century, Florence was one of the main centres of the Mannerist movement. These artists endeavoured to study the nature of art itself and made formal and technical perfection a necessary implication of their art and replaced idealistic contents with intellectualistic complexity. Francesco Granacci was one of the Florentine Mannerists who spent most of their time in debating whether Leonardo, Michelangelo or Raphael was the greatest Master.

Madonna and Child, by *Alonso Berruguete*.

This panel – painted c. 1517 – was for some time attributed to Rosso Fiorentino, but critics agree that it probably belongs to the later production of the Spanish painter. The composition manages to combine early 15th century tenets with Michelangelesque innovations.

Above: **Madonna and Child, by Alonso Berruguete**; *below*: **Visitation, by Mariotto Albertinelli.**

Above: **Portrait of a lady, by Giuliano Bugiardini and Apparition of the Virgin to St. Bernard, by Fra' Bartolomeo;** *below*: **Christ before Caiaphas, by Bachiacca and Moses defending the daughters of Jethro, by Rosso Fiorentino.**

ROOM 26
(Raphael and Andrea del Sarto)

Raphael was born in Urbino on the 6th April 1483. His father, Giovanni Santi, was court painter at the Montefeltro court and compiled some Chronicles of interest to students of 15th century art. The precocious talents of young Raphael were immediately put to work in the workshop of the most famous painter of the area: Pietro Perugino of Perugia. Once he had mastered the elegant, composed manner of his Umbrian master, Raphael moved to Florence, where he inevitably came into contact with the diatribe between Leonardo and Michelangelo, who were both partisans, although on diverging levels, of the concept of art as an instrument of knowledge. Raphael took neither one side nor the other, but decided to place his art at the service of the recognized Truth and religous dogma. He spent four years in Florence, painting the Madonnas which were to be his most successful genre. Although he maintained his stylistic independence, Raphael was an attentive observer of the two great masters, copying detail and figures from both masters with passionate assiduity. In 1508 he went to Rome, whereupon, Pope Julius II, having been given proof of his ability, decided to assign him the commission for the frescoes of the Vatican rooms (Stanze) sending a whole group of other artists, who had been working on the project, packing . In his Dispute on the Sacrament, in the School of Athens and in the Freeing of Peter, Raphael provided entrancing examples of his felicitously evocative, narrative powers. It was in these years that his classical perfection of style was at its height (exemplified by the Sistine Madonna (in Dresden), the Madonna of the Chair (Pitti Palace-Florence) and the Transfiguration (Vatican). Among his non-religiously inspired works, one should recall the mythological frescoes in the Farnesina Palace (Rome) and the Roman villa of his patron Agostino Chigi. He died in 1520 aged barely 37, but already immensely famous and revered by countless admiring followers: a veritable forerunner of European Mannerism.

Above: **Self-portrait, by Raphael**; *below*: **Portrait of (?) Francesco Maria della Rovere**; *opposite*: **the well-known Madonna of the Goldfinch, both by Raphael.**

Portrait of Pietro Carnesecchi, by *Domenico Puligo*.

Martyrdom of St. Maurice and the 11,000 Martyrs, by Jacopo Carrucci known as *Pontormo*.

Sts. Michael, John Gualbert, John the Baptist, Bernardo degli Uberti, by *Andrea del Sarto*.

Known as the Altarpiece of the Four Saints. The predella shows scenes from their lives.

Portrait of a woman with a basket of spindles, by Jacopo Carrucci known as *Pontormo*.

Portrait of unknown, by Jacopo Carrucci known as *Pontormo*.

Portrait of Pope Julius II, by *Raphael and his workshop*.

Leo X and Cardinals Giulio de' Medici and Luigi de' Rossi, by *Raphael*, c. 1519.

In this late work, Raphael conveys the same warm, luminous feeling present in all his work. The new elements are a richer

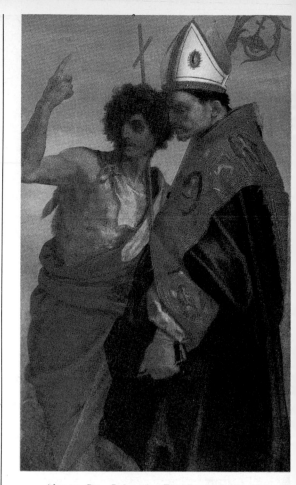

palette, a result of the influence of Venetian school colourism, and a greater psychological insight.

Madonna of the Goldfinch, by *Raphael*, 1506.

This is one of the first paintings that Raphael, a native of Urbino, painted in Florence. Contact with the Florentine painters caused Raphael to move beyond his early phase, wholly dominated by the influence of his teacher Perugino, and assimilate the teachings of Leonardo, whose characteristic pyramidal composition is apparent in this work. Raphael has painstakingly avoided all tension and jarring notes in this panel endowing it with a gentle charm. His figures are modelled with the same delicacy, and the warm tenderness of the family scene is enhanced by the soft colours of the landscape, that seems to partake of the intimate atmosphere.

Portrait of Francesco Maria della Rovere, by *Raphael*, c. 1504.

Self-portrait, by *Raphael*, c. 1508.

St. Anthony Abbot, by Jacopo Carrucci known as *Pontormo*.

Madonna and Child enthroned with Sts. Francis and John the Evangelist, by *Andrea del Sarto*.

This panel commonly known as the *Madonna delle Arpie*, from the Harpies sculpted on the base of the Virgin's throne was painted in 1517 for the Monastery of San Francis in Florence. Vasari praised Andrea del Sarto as «painter without fault» because of the perfection of his drawing, purity of colour, and harmony of composition. The Michelangelesque monumentality of the figures is softened by the warm, «sfumato» colours, reminiscent of Raphael. From an iconographic viewpoint, the Madonna recalls the Fra Bartolommeo and Mariotto Albertinelli Virgins, whereas the figure of St. John, according to Vasari, is copied from Sansovino. Some critics even think that the St. John is an actual portrait of the artist and the Madonna a likeness of the painter's wife Lucrezia. In the church of Santa Maria della Croce al Tempio in Florence, it was replaced by a copy by Francesco Petrucci.

St. James and the two boys, by *Andrea del Sarto*.

This work belongs to the last phase of Andrea's career. In 1529, the painter joined the Company of San Jacopo del Nicchio and painted its standard choosing these very figures as his subject: St. James with two young boys at his feet in the habits of the «battuti» (flagellant monks). The painting proposes an original solution to the expressive problems posed by a religious spirit thrown into turmoil by the chaotic upheaval of the Reform and foreshadows the Counter-Reformistic spirit that characterizes the paintings of the second half of the 16th century. Biographical details relating to the artist come to us once again from Vasari who happened to be one of his pupils. Andrea probably owed his name to the profession of his father, who was, in fact, a taylor (sarto) all his life. After attending Piero di Cosimo's workshop as an adolescent, he ran away from his master, exasperated by his odd behaviour, and decided to follow the teachings of Franciabigio and Fra Bartolommeo, as well as being much impressed by Michelangelo and Leonardo.

Above: **Sts. John the Baptist and St. Bernard degli Uberti, by Andrea del Sarto;** *below*: **Portrait of Woman with a basket of spindles, by Pontormo.**

Above: **St. Michael, St. John Gualberto and the famous Madonna of the Harpies, by Andrea del Sarto;** *below*: **Portrait of Unknown, by Pontormo; detail showing two Angels, from the Altarpiece of the Four Saints, by Andrea del Sarto and Leo X between two Cardinals, by Raphael.**

ROOM 27
(Pontormo)

Born in Empoli, in 1494, Jacopo Carrucci, known as Pontormo, is one of the most important Florentine Mannerist artist and certainly the most restless and tormented. Vasari and the invaluable diary the painter kept during the last years of his life are the main sources of information we have on his life and work. He was a loner, an unsociable, permanently dissatisfied character. A pupil of Andrea del Sarto, he led his master's teachings one step further in an exhausting search after formal beauty that was no longer founded on composure and balance, but on movement.

Portrait of a youth with gloves, by *Franciabigio*.

Holy Family, by *Agnolo Bronzino*.

Supper at Emmaus, by J. Carrucci known as *Pontormo*, 1525.
Pontormo, together with Rosso Fiorentino, was the leader of the Florentine Mannerist school, and was known for his introverted, melancholy character, although he was open to changes in taste and constantly on the lookout for new models to study. This particular work reveals a strong Dürer influence, and is characterized by a breathless feeling of suspended animation epitomised in Christ's slow gesture. Around the humble table and the three seated figures, several Carthusian monks can be made out in the background. Their presence is due to the fact that the work was commissioned for the Charterhouse of Galluzzo where Pontormo had fled from the plague then raging in Florence.

Lament over the Dead Christ, by *Agnolo Bronzino*, 1525.

Birth of St. John the Baptist, by Jacopo Carrucci known as *Pontormo*, 1526.(Delivery basin)

Madonna and Child enthroned with Sts. John the Baptist, Anthony Abbot, Jerome, and Stephen, by *Rosso Fiorentino*, c. 1528.

Portrait of the musician Francesco dell'Ajolle, by Jacopo Carrucci, known as *Pontormo*.

Madonna and Child with St. John the Baptist, by *Jacopino del Conte*.

Portrait of Maria Salviati (?), by J. Carrucci known as *Pontormo*.

Adoration of the Shepherds, attribuited to *Giorgio Vasari*.

Portrait of a gentlewoman, by *Agnolo Bronzino*.

Portrait of a girl, by *Rosso Fiorentino*.

Holy Family, by *Domenico Beccafumi*.

Three episodes from the life of St. Acacio, by Francesco Ubertini known as *Bachiacca*.

Deposition, by *Francesco Ubertini* known as *Bachiacca*.

Madonna and Child with Angels and Sts. Jerome and Francis, by Jacopo Carrucci known as *Pontormo*.

Above: **Madonna and Child with Angels and Saints, by Pontormo;** *below*: **Birth of St. John the Baptist, by Pontormo and Holy Family, by Domenico Beccafumi.**

Above: detail of Adoration of the Shepherds, attrib. to G. Vasari and Supper at Emmaus, by Pontormo; *below*: Episode from the Life of St. Acacio, by Bachiacca.

ROOM 28
(Titian)

At the beginning of the 16th century, Venice was at the height of its splendour. The art of painting flourished in a cultured, erudite, cosmopolitan atmosphere achieving a position of eminence among the arts thanks to novel technical and theoretical solutions. The importance of tonal values, Giorgione's novel use of light, to a certain extent already discernible in Bellini's later work and, according to Vasari attributable to Leonardo's brief visit to Venice in 1501, was to mark a whole generation of artists. Titian, a pupil of Giorgione, possessed himself of his master's techniques and used them to express his own powerfully original personality. Throughout his long, successful life, admired by the common folk, as well as by the most powerful rulers (including François I, Charles V and Philip II) he continued to renew and enrich both his technique and style. As in Giorgione, Titian's forms are given body without being enslaved by line, although, unlike his master's works, the harmony of the composition is due to the play of light and shade and not to Giorgione's subtle chromatic choice that envelops everything in softly blended, meditative halftones. His Manneristic contacts are also apparent, as well as a rich neo-Platonic heritage; his dominant features are his warm palette, classical, monumental qualities and his use of massed colour in shaping space and figures.

Portrait of Caterina Cornaro, old copy of a *Titian* original.

Flora, by Tiziano Vercellio known as *Titian*, c. 1515.

This early work by Titian is one of his most popular. It shows strong Giorgionesque influences; the painting nevertheless reveals Titian's love for rounded fleshy figures and intense colours, that always characterized his work.

Venus of Urbino, by *Titian*, 1538.

Titian is the indisputed master of an entire century of Venetian painting (which in turn was the leading Italian school of the 16th century), countering Mannerism's intellectual refinement and draughtsmanship-oriented painting with a burst of colouristic virtuosity. One of the masterpieces turned out at the height of Titian's artistic maturity, this painting was commissioned by the Duke of Urbino, Guidobaldo della Rovere. Titian's extraordinary technical skill is revealed in the warm flesh tones and glowing palette. A masterful touch is the placing of the two female figures, maids, in the background to convey a feeling of realistic intimacy. The prototype for the reclining Venus is Giorgione's version, now in the Gemäldegalerie of Dresden, but Titian's rendition reveals a plastic sense and sensuality lacking in Giorgione.

Knight of Malta, by *Titian*, c. 1518.

Up to very recently, critics thought this was a portrait of Stefano Colonna, but recently serious doubts have been advanced as to this identification. The inscription on the back of the panel says «Giorgio da Castelfranco d(ett)o Giorgione». The attribution to Titian is in fact very questionable and only an accurate restoration will be able to solve the problem satisfactorily.

Above: **Knight of Malta, by Titian;** *below*: **Portrait of Caterina Cornaro, by Titian.**

Above: the famous Venus of Urbino; *below*: Flora and Eleonora Gonzaga della Rovere – three splendid works by Titian.

Judith, by *Jacopo Palma the Elder*.

Palma the Elder was one of Giorgione's followers who was also affected by Titian's early style; he adopted the manner of the latter, bathing the whole painting in golden suffused light.

Portrait of Eleonora Gonzaga della Rovere, Duchess of Urbino, by *Titian*.

This portrait was probably painted in 1537, when the Duchess was staying in Venice, which would seem to be confirmed by a contemporary document that records the painting as already in Pesaro in 1538.

Portrait of Francesco Maria della Rovere, Duke of Urbino, by *Titian*.

This portrait was signed twice, once in Latin and once in the «vulgar» (Venetian? Italian) tongue. The Uffizi collection also possesses a full-length sketch of the Duke in the same dress, which has led certain critics to believe that the canvas was cut, whereas others think that Titian abandoned the idea of a full-length portrait, choosing the half-figure solution instead, so that the Duke's portrait would be symmetrical with the likeness of his noble consort.

Portrait of Raffaele Grassi, by *Sebastiano Florigerio*.

Raffaele Grassi was the father of Giambattista, painter and architect, known to Vasari, who mentions the latter extensively in his «Lives of the Artists».

Portrait of the physician Coignati, by *Paolo Pino*.

Pino is probably more renowned for his treatise on painting than for his actual painting skills. This is one of the few works that can be attributed to him without any doubt.

Resurrection of Lazarus, by *Jacopo Palma il Vecchio*.

Two different replicas of this painting have come down to us: one is in the Uffizi, the other in Philadelphia. A 17th century print seems to hint that Palma may have painted a third version, now lost.

Holy Family with Sts. John the Baptist and Mary Magdalen, by *Jacopo Palma the Elder*.

A 17th century print indicates that the original dimensions of the painting were different to the present ones. The panel shows evident signs of having been worked on by more than one hand in the Master's workshop and is dated c. 1520.

Portrait of a man, by *Francesco Beccaruzzi*.

Variously attributed, it bears on old inscription that says «Rosso del Pordenone», but critics were long in favour of Palma the Elder, before the Beccaruzzi hypothesis prevailed.

Venus and Cupid, by *Titian*.

Some critics attribute at least part of the picture to Titian's workshop. Iconographically, the reclining Venus recalls a classical attitude much used in antiquity, as well as recalling the *Venus and Eros* by Michelangelo.

Portrait of Bishop Ludovico Beccadelli, by *Titian*.

Above: **Judith, by Palma the Elder;** *below*: **Portrait of Bishop Ludovico Beccadelli, by Titian.**

Above: **Holy Family with Saints John the Baptist and Mary Magdalen, by Palma the Elder;** *below*:
Venus and Cupid, by Titian.

ROOM 29
(Parmigianino and Central Italian Mannerism)

Mannerism spread through Aemilia in the train of a tradition of intense religious sentimentality. Correggio and Parmigianino breathed new life into this rather cooped-up atmosphere. The former drew on Mantegna's works in Mantua, the latter harked back chiefly to Raphael. A restless, odd character, Parmigianino was soon charmed away from painting by his fascination for alchemy, which he devoted himself to with such abandon that he neglected his commissions. In 1539 he had the important contract for a series of frescoes in the church of the Steccata in Parma taken away from him because he had not fulfilled his contractual obligations; very depressed, he retired to Casalmaggiore, where he died aged barely 37 years old.

Jesus on His Way to Calvary, by *Battista Franco*.

Massacre of the Innocents, by *Amico Aspertini*.

Adoration of the Shepherds, by *Amico Aspertini*.

Martha and Mary before the Saviour, by *Girolamo da Carpi*.

Adoration of the Child, by *Ludovico Mazzolino*.

Judgment of Zaleucus, by *Perin del Vaga*.

Noli me tangere, by *Lavinia Fontana*.

Madonna and Child with Saints, by Francesco Mazzola known as *Parmigianino*, c. 1530.

Portrait of an unknown man, by Francesco Mazzola known as *Parmigianino*.

Madonna of the long neck, by Francesco Mazzola known as *Parmigianino*.

A leader of the Aemilian Mannerist school, Parmigianino worked on this painting from 1534 to the year of his death in 1540. The *Madonna dal Collo Lungo* (long neck), undoubtedly his best-known work, lays a greater emphasis on the profane rather than the sacred, the elegance of the figures' elongated limbs culminates in the splendid face of the Madonna. In contrast to the worldly group of foreground figures, the ascetic figure of a prophet unwinds a scroll in the background of the lower righthand corner.

Annunciation, by Benvenuto Tisi known as *Garofalo*.

The Judgment of Paris, by Ippolito Scarsella known as *Scarsellino*.

Tarquinius the Proud founding the Temple of Jupiter on Capitol Hill, by *Perin del Vaga*.

Madonna and Child, by *Luca Cambiaso*.

Clelia and the virgins fleeing from the field of Posenna, by *Domenico Beccafumi*.

Adoration of the Child, by *Girolamo da Carpi*.

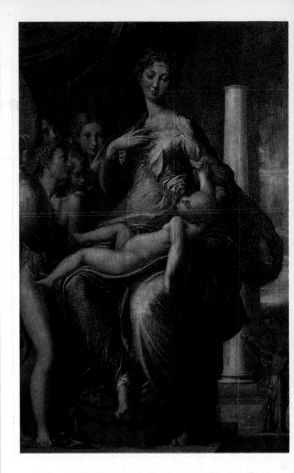

Above: **Madonna of the long neck, by Parmigianino;** *below*: **detail from Christ with the tribute money, by Garofalo (Room 30).**

Above: **Jesus on His way to Calvary, by Battista Franco;** below: **Rest on the flight to Egypt, by Dosso Dossi** (Room 30).

Above: **Adoration of the Shepherds, by Amico Aspertini;** below: **Noli me tangere, by Lavinia Fontana.**

ROOM 30
(Aemilian School)

The numerous lesser Aemilian artists of the 15th century maintain a fairly provincial level, with the possible exception of Garofalo and of the «Northerner» Mazzolino. Dosso Dossi is also not to be included in the general rule.

Circumcision, by *Ludovico Mazzolino*.

Christ with the Tribute money, by Benvenuto Tisi known as *Garofalo*.
Copy of a Titian.

Rest on the flight to Egypt, by *Dosso Dossi*.

Vision of St. Hildegard, by *Battista Dossi*.

Portrait of a youth, by *Niccolò dell'Abate* (also attributed to *Parmigianino*).

Madonna and Child with St. John the Baptist, by *Nicola Pisano*.

Madonna and St. Anne of the cherries, by *Ludovico Mazzolino*.

ROOM 31
(Dosso Dossi)

Master of the bizarre, magic and fanciful, Giovanni Luteri, known as Dosso Dossi, was born in Ferrara c. 1479 and died in 1542. His contacts with Titian and the Giorgione entourage in general, as well as with Ariosto and his «Orlando Furioso», exercised a decisive effect on his career. Dosso's painting is highly inventive, pleasing and as surprising as a fairy-story.

Head of a youth, by *Lorenzo Lotto*, c. 1505.

Madonna in Glory, by *Dosso Dossi*.

Portrait of a Warrior, by *Dosso Dossi*.

Portrait of a woman, by *Sebastiano del Piombo*, 1512.
Traditionally this painting is known as «La Fornarina» (the baker's girl), although the sitter is not in the same woman who often sat for Raphael, to whom it was long attributed.

Witchcraft, by *Dosso Dossi*.
This painting reveals the artist's characteristic style: bright colour and lively composition, and emphatic contrast of light and shade. It has an especially magical and somewhat grotesque feeling, well-suited to this particular work whose mysterious subject is yet unknown (one theory is that it shows the casting of a magic spell intended to make two people fall in love).

Sick man, attributed to *Sebastiano del Piombo*, 1514.

Head of an old man, 16th century Venetian school.

Above: **Head of old man, 16th century Venetian School;** *below*: **Sick man, attrib. to Sebastiano del Piombo.**

Above: **Witchcraft**; *below*: **Portrait of a Warrior, both by Dosso Dossi.**

Above: **Madonna in Glory, by Dosso Dossi;** *below*: **the «Fornarina», by Sebastiano del Piombo.**

ROOM 32
(16th century Venetian School)

In 16th century Venice, the great artists of the calibre of Giorgione and Titian (we will discuss the effects exercised by Tintoretto and Veronese further on) foster the development of a large number of young painters, each possessed of his own individual traits, but all partaking in some way of the themes or modes of their masters.

Sacra Conversazione, by *Lorenzo Lotto*, 1534.

Lorenzo Lotto, a Venetian painter whose artistic formation was neverthless extemely complex, must be regarded as a loner, who was mostly untouched by the mainstream of Venetian art of his day, primarily influenced by Titian and Giorgione. This painting is an example of how Lotto blends Venetian colourism with Roman and Düreresque elements.

Portrait of a boy, by *Girolamo Romanino*.

Portrait of a man, by *Girolamo Muziano*.

Portrait of a man with fur collar, by *Paris Bordone*.

Death of Adonis, by *Sebastiano del Piombo*, c. 1512.

Although Sebastiano del Piombo received his training in the Venetian school, in 1510 he moved to Rome where he came into contact with a cultural milieu dominated by Raphael and Michelangelo. This remarkable painting is a prime example of how he managed to blend two opposite traditions: the solidly-built, fleshy figures, exuding warmth and exuberance, recline languidly against a landscape that includes a hazy view of Venice in the background.

Portrait of a man, by *Paris Bordone*.

Paris Bordone belongs to the group of Venetian artist who tried to blend local colourism with the draftsmanship of Central Italian Mannerism. His two portraits in this room are full of symbolism. More particularly the portrait of a knight (with jousting helm and lance) is to be interpreted as a veritable love message, addressed to the unknown lady, for whom the portrait was painted: a little Cupid in the background is about to deliver a letter to a lady and various objects, such as a ring and a garland of flowers lie on the table beside the helm, hint at an amorous relationship. The second portrait (the man with the fur collar) was probably a youthful work and has also been attributed to Bernardino Licinio.

Portrait of Teofilo Folengo, by *Girolamo Romanino*.

Susanna and the Elders, by *Lorenzo Lotto*.

Madonna and Child with St. Francis, by *Bernardino Licinio*.

Portrait of a man, by *Domenico Campagnola*.

Bathsheba at her bath, by *Domenico Brusasorci*.

Portrait of a man, Venetian School, 2nd half of the 16th century.

Portrait of Unknown, by *Alessandro Oliverio*.

Above: **Portrait of Unknown, by Alessandro Oliverio**; *below*: **Susanna and the old men, by Lorenzo Lotto.**

Above: **Death of Adonis, by Sebastiano del Piombo;** *below*: **Portrait of a man with fur collar, by Paris Bordone and Bathsheba at her bath, by Domenico Brusasorci.**

ROOM 33
(16th century Corridor)

Works by Italian and non-Italian painters, full of felicitous inventiveness and technical ability, which are a rich documentation of the «less» important art in circulation in the 16th century, hang along the walls of this passage-way. The many patrons who commissioned these paintings, belonged to the ruling classes of the time, sharing the same refined tastes and culture.

Portrait of a lady, attributed to *Jean Perréal*.

Portrait of King François I of France, by *François Clouet*.

The portrait dated c. 1540, was probably part of the dowry of Christine of Lorraine grand-daughter to Catherine de' Medici, the famous queen of France, married to Henri II whose portrait, also by Clouet, hangs in this passage. François Clouet, son to the painter Jean, was born in Tours c. 1510. In the wake of his father, he became a member of the so-called School of Fontanebleau, which comprised the painters of the court of François I, king of France. The latter was an enthusiastic admirer and patron of Italian art and adored gathering aound him the great Florentine masters of the 16th century such as Leonardo da Vinci, Benvenuto Cellini and Rosso Fiorentino, as well as being profoundly attracted to the Venetian art of Titian and Giorgione. A considerable group of French artists succumbed to the attractions of these great masters, producing an extremely «courtly», refined type of art that seemed to gravitate naturally towards mythological subjects and richly decorated work.

Christ carrying the cross, by *Luis de Morales*.

Portrait of Viglius van Aytta, by *Frans Pourbus the Elder*.

Viglius van Aytta of Zwichem, was a Dutch lawyer, an intellectual, a friend of Erasmus of Rotterdam and an imperial envoy. He was one of the artist's best patrons. The portraits seems to have been painted c. 1566. Frans Pourbus the Elder was one of the numerous Dutch artists who dedicated most of their efforts to portrait-panting and keeping the lively, realistic attitude of the Flemish tradition alive throughout the 16th century.

Self-portrait, by *Antonio Moro*.

Portrait of Cornelius Gros, by *Christoph Amberger*.

Portrait of a man in armour, by *16th century French School, 1589*.

Portrait of Christine of Lorraine *French School, F. Clouet (?)*

Portrait of Torquato Tasso, by *Alessandro Allori*.

Sacrifice of Isaac, by Jacopo Chimenti known as *Empoli*.

Drunkenness of Noah, by Jacopo Chimenti known as *Empoli*.

Medusa head, 16th century Flemish school.

St. Peter walking on the waters, by *Alessandro Allori*, 1606.

Above: **Portrait of Cornelius Gros, by Christoph Amberger;** *below*: **Sacrifice of Isaac, by Jacopo Chimenti.**

Above: **Portrait of Viglius van Aytta, by Frans Pourbus the Elder and Portrait of François I of France, by François Clouet;** *below*: **Medusa head, 16th century Flemish School.**

ROOM 33 *continued*

Lament over the dead Christ, by *Agnolo Bronzino*.

Sacrifice of Isaac, by *Alessandro Allori*, 1601.

Allori was a late mannerist painter and enjoyed considerable fame in his lifetime, thanks chiefly to his eclectic spirit. This *Sacrifice* can be classed amongst his latest works, due to the obvious Flemish traits he reveals in his detailed rendering of the landscape which characterize Florentine art during Alessandro's last years. His composition reveals a painstaking adherence to Counter-Reformation precepts, whereby every single episode of the Biblical story is pedantically illustrated.

Allegory of Happiness, by *Agnolo Bronzino*, c. 1570.

Venus and Cupid, by *Alessandro Allori*.

Susanna at her bath, by *Gregorio Pagani (also attributed to Orazio Samacchini)*.

The Three Graces, by F. Morandini known as *Poppi*.

Joseph and Potiphar's wife, by *Gregorio Pagani (*also attributed to *Orazio Samacchini)*.

Vulcan's forge, by *Giorgio Vasari*.

Intellectual and man of the world, painter, architect and writer, Giorgio Vasari of Arezzo (1511-1574) was educated in the Mannerist mode in Andrea del Sarto's workshop. In 1538 he was in Rome and haunted the workshop of Michelangelo who advised him to devote himself to architecture. It was in effect in the latter field that he was to enjoy most success, when he built the Uffizi. As regards painting, his most important project was the series of frescoes in Palazzo Vecchio. Vasari's fame, however, rests almost exclusively on his compilation of the *Lives of the Artists* of his time (first edition 1550), arranged as if the historical progress of art were to be viewed as a succession of three ages: infancy – from Cimabue to the end of the 14th century; youth – the 15th century and maturity – the era of Michelangelo. His Lives are still a vital source of critical comments, biographical information and a testimony of the taste of a period.

Fortune, by *Jacopo Ligozzi*.

Hercules and the Muses, by *Alessandro Allori*.

The Iron Age, by *Jacopo Zucchi*.

The Silver Age, by *Jacopo Zucchi*.

The Golden Age, by *Jacopo Zucchi*.

Portrait of a lady, by *Alessandro Allori*.
On the back is the Allegory of Life.

Country Dance, by *Marten van Valckenborch*.

St. Sebastian, by *Andrea Boscoli*.

Sacrifice of Isaac, by *Jacopo Ligozzi*.

Arthemisia mourning Mausoleus, by Francesco Rossi known as *Cecchino Salviati*.

Above: **The Golden Age, by Jacopo Zucchi;** *below*: **Fortune, by Jacopo Ligozzi.**

Above: **Sacrifice of Isaac, by Alessandro Allori;** *below*: **Allegory of Happiness, by Agnolo Bronzino and Venus and Cupid, by Alessandro Allori.**

ROOM 34
(Veronese)

Paolo Caliari, known as Veronese, from the town where he was born in 1528, as son of Gabriele, a stone-carver was trained as a painter in the workshop of Caroto, exposed to the Aemilian-Lombard Mannerist influences. Towards the middle of the century, he was summoned to Venice and commissioned to decorate some of the halls in the Doges' Palace: his name was made. His luminous colour, his pleasing tonal combinations, his compositional facility caused him to be much in demand all over the Veneto: churches and patrician villas vying for his spacious scenographic paintings on religious themes, which manage to break away from the prevailing Counter-Reformation conformist tenets.

St. Agatha crowned by angels, by *Paolo Veronese*.

Portrait of unknown, by *Giulio Campi*.

Esther and Ahasuerus, school of *Veronese*.

Guitar-player, by *Giulio Campi*.

Portrait of a man, by *Jacopo Tintoretto*, 1546.

Portrait of unknown man with a book, by *Giovan Battista Moroni*, 1563.

Portrait of Court Pietro Secco-Suardo, by *G. B. Moroni*.

Giovan Battista Moroni, a native of Bergamo, studied under Moretto, leader of the Lombard school known as «*verismo*». Unlike his contemporary Bronzino, whose refined portraits are of high-ranking courtly figures, Moroni numbered Lombards belonging to the upper and lower bourgeois classes among his sitters and produced realistic pictures of their simple, austere world, sometimes with allegorical allusions, depicted in a constantly and convincingly unostentatious fashion.

Portrait of Galeazzo Campi, the artist's father, by *Giulio Campi*.

Martyrdom of St. Justine, by *Paolo Veronese*.

Annunciation, by *Paolo Veronese*.

Portrait of Giovanni Antonio Pantera, by *G. B. Moroni*.

The Transfiguration, by *Giovanni Girolamo Savoldo*.

Holy Family with St. Barbara, by *Paolo Veronese*.

Veronese along with Titian and Tintoretto, is one of the key figures in the development of 16th century Venetian painting. His style hinges on a solid decorative skill and his remarkable ability to fill huge spaces with complex scenes. Veronese is famous for his bright colours, elaborately-costumed figures, and his way of depicting the magnificently opulent society of 16th century Venice. Unlike Titian, Veronese does not achieve his colouristic effects by mixing his colours: he places one shade of his incredibly rich palette next to the other, so that each tint gleams with its own splendour. In this late painting of a religious subject, Veronese has chosen a quieter, more intimate tone.

Above: **Portrait of Count Pietro Secco – Suardo, by G.B. Moroni;** *below*: **Angel from Annunciation, by Paolo Veronese.**

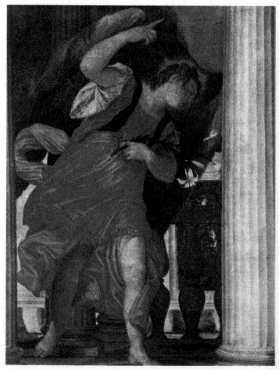

Above: **Esther and Ahasuerus, by Paolo Veronese's Circle;** *below*: **Annunciate Virgin, from the Annunciation and Holy Family with St. Barbara, both by Paolo Veronese.**

ROOM 35
(Tintoretto and Barocci)

Jacopo was born in Venice, towards 1519, as son of Giovanni Battista Robusti, a silk-dyer (tintore = dyer) from Lucca. He had an introverted personality and travelled very little (unlike many of his contemporaries): he went once to Mantua and once, perhaps, to Rome, spending the rest of his life in Venice. Michelangelo was the artist Tintoretto was most interested in. He was a pupil of Titian's for a short while, but did not get on very well with him: the master's jealousy and the pupil's awkward personality made the apprenticeship difficult. Tintoretto attempted to capture the effect of movement in the visualisation of a fleeting instant. His composition is never constrained, his style is dynamic and he uses light to dazzle causing contours to disappear. The painting of Federico Barocci (of Urbino) reveals totally different limitations. He was a representative of the late Mannerist current, that was turning away from Michelangelo and cleaving to Raphael and Correggio. His objectives are clearly those of the educationally oriented Counter-Reformation religious propaganda.

The Samaritan Woman at the Well, by Jacopo Robusti known as *Tintoretto*.

Portrait of the artist, by *Jacopo Bassano*.

Christ at the Well, by Jacopo Robusti known as *Tintoretto*.
The Christ at the well and the Samaritan woman panels used to belong to the organ of the church of San Benedetto in Venice. They are generally dated 1560 or 1575-1588.

Ecce Homo, by *Joachim Benckelaer*, 1566.

Portrait of a lady, by *Federico Barocci*.

Portrait of red-headed man, by J. Robusti known as *Tintoretto*.

Portrait of an admiral, by *Tintoretto*.

Noli me tangere, by *Federico Barocci*, 1590.

St. Francis receiving the Stigmata, by Ludovico Cardi known as *Cigoli*.

Portrait of Francesco Maria II della Rovere, by *Federico Barocci*.

Apparition of St. Augustine, by *Domenico Tintoretto*.

Sts. John the Evangelist and Francis, by *El Greco*.
Domenikos Theotocopoulos, born in Crete in 1541, was a pupil of Titian in Venice c. 1560, where his style becomes more colouristic and he is also led to adopt Tintorettesque chiaro-scuro vibrations. In 1565 he moved to Toledo, where he acquired the nickname of El Greco. The Venetian foundations of his style transpire from his elongated forms and tragic, passionate atmospheres, expressing the artist's profound mysticism.

Story of Joseph, by *Jacopo Bassano*.

Above: detail from the Apparition of St. Augustine, by D. Tintoretto; *below*: St. Francis receiving the Stigmata, by Ludovico Ciardi.

Above: Leda and the Swan; *below*: Christ at the well and the Samaritan Woman, three splendid works by Tintoretto.

ROOM 35 *continued*

Family concert, by *Leandro Bassano*.

Madonna of the People, by *Federico Barocci*.
Painted between 1575 and 1579 for the Lay Fraternity of Pieve di Arezzo. The painting is generally considered this Central Italian Mannerist artist's masterpiece combining the draftsmanship of the Roman and Tuscan schools with Venetian colourism. The subjects of his painting are mostly religious and sentimental.

Annunciation to the Shepherds, by *Jacopo Bassano*.

Wedding at Cana, by *Andrea Boscoli*.

Portrait of Jacopo Sansovino, by Jacopo Robusti known as *Tintoretto*, 1566.

Portrait of an old man with a fur trimmed coat, attributed to Jacopo Robusti known as *Tintoretto*.

St. Francis receiving the Stigmata, by *Federico Barocci*, c. 1595.
Copy of the panel commissioned by the Urbino Franciscan monks.

Leda and the Swan, by J. Robusti known as *Tintoretto*, c. 1570.
In Tintoretto, Central Italian Mannerism blends into the Venetian tradition. The composition, as in this late work with Leda, is never static, never symmetrical, never restful.

Portrait of Ippolito della Rovere (?) by *Federico Barocci*.

St. Margaret, by *Jacopo Palma the Younger*.

Portrait of the poet Giulio Strozzi, by *Tiberio Tinelli*.

The burning bush, by *Jacopo Bassano*.

Two hunting dogs, by *Jacopo Bassano*.

Portrait of a gentleman, attributed to *Tintoretto*.

EXIT HALL

Since Bernardo Buontalenti's original staircase was re-opened, rooms 36 through 40 were eliminated and this hall has been restored.

Balthazar's feast, by *Giovanni Martinelli*.

Wild boar, Roman copy of a 3rd century B.C. Hellenistic original.
This is a marble replica of the original bronze. In 1612 Pietro Tacca used it as his model for the Boar Fountain in the Straw Market.

Angelica and Medorus, by *Orazio Fidani*.

Torso of a satyr, Pergamon, 2nd century B.C.

Above: **Portrait of Francesco Maria della Rovere**, by Federico Barrocci; *below*: **3rd century B.C. Wild Boar (Exit Hall)**.

Above: **St. John the Evangelist and St. Francis, by El Greco;** *below*: **Madonna of the People, by Federico Barocci.**

Above: **Noli me tangere, by Federico Barocci;** *below*: **Wedding at Cana, by Andrea Boscoli.**

ROOM 41
(Rubens and Van Dyck)

Above: **Portrait of Charles V, by Antonis van Dyck**; *below*: **Portrait of Galileo Galilei, by Justus Sustermans.**

Pieter Paul Rubens was the first, great, fully international artist, whose life was in total unison with the historical events of his time. He was an untiring traveller and the courts of Europe vied with each other for his services. He was an able diplomat and was engaged in many complex and important political negotiations; as well as maintaining a constant search after knowledge, thus impersonating the ideal all-round late-Renaissance/early Baroque man with his organic vision. He was born in Siegen (Germany) on the 28th June 1577 and moved with his mother, fairly early on, to his family's home-town, Antwerp, in the Netherlands, where he learnt the rudiments of painting in the workshop of Otto van Veen. He went to Italy on his first journey in search of knowledge. In 1600 we find him at the Gonzaga court in Mantua; this is also where he commenced his diplomatic career. He then moved to Genoa and Rome, absorbing new pictorial ideas and taking into account both past and present trends. He thus blends Michelangelo's monumental qualities with the gleaming colours of Titian and Veronese, the draftsmanship of Raphael with Northern European expressionism and Düreresque rigour. It was his eclectic nature, together with his extraordinary talent and very up-to-date capacity in managing his work that gave him his truly international success. He received commissions from the Belgian Archduke and Archduchess Albert and Isabella, from Maria de' Medici, Queen Regent of France, from Philip IV of Spain and from Charles I of England. In 1609, he married Isabella Brandt. His workshop grew in size and he was joined by one of his most famous pupils: Antonis van Dyck. At the age of 53 (his wife had died four years earlier) he married the 16 year-old Hélène Fourment. He died of gout, ten years later, in 1640.

Ferdinand of Spain, the Cardinal Infante, triumphantly entering Antwerp, *Jan van der Hoecke.*

Portrait of an old woman, by *Jacob Jordaens.*

Henry IV of France triumphantly entering Paris, by *Pieter Paul Rubens.*

Rubens, was constantly in contact with the Italian, especially Venetian, artists of his day. His imposing canvases are animated by an intense vitality deriving from a masterful juxtaposition of dynamic composition and an extraordinarily lively palette. In this painting and its companion piece showing Henry IV at the Battle of Ivry, Rubens gives free rein to his incredible skill in organizing huge complex compositions into a harmonious whole. They convey an effect which is at the same time a bit rhetorical and over-done, in keeping with the elaborate tastes of the court of Maria de' Medici, Queen of France, who commissioned the paintings in 1628.

Portrait of Isabella Brandt, by *Pieter Paul Rubens.*

Isabella Brandt, Rubens' first wife, sat for the portrait around 1620. The blended colours and fleshy, well-rounded figure are typical of the painter's style.

Portrait of Margaret of Lorraine, by *Antonis Van Dyck.*

Above: **Henri IV at the Battle of Ivry, by P.P. Rubens;** *below*: **Portrait of Isabella Brandt and Portrait of Philip IV of Spain, both by P.P. Rubens.**

Portrait of Philip IV of Spain, school of *P. P.Rubens*.

Portrait of Emperor Charles V, by *Antonis Van Dyck*.

Portrait of Galileo Galilei, by *Justus Sustermans*, c. 1636.
Justus Sustermans, or Suttermans (1597-1681) was trained in the workshop of the Flemish artist Willem de Vos, and dedicated his whole career to portrait-painting, receiving commissions from all over Europe. As from 1620, he worked in Florence for the Medici court. Galileo Galilei's portrait was painted in 1636 for the Pisan astronomer and mathematician himself, as a present for a French admirer of Galileo's. It entered the grand-ducal collections in 1643 when it was brought back from Paris.

Henry IV at the Battle of Ivry, by *P.P Rubens*, c. 1628.

Portrait of Justus Sustermans' mother, by *A. Van Dyck*.

Bacchanal, school of *Pieter Paul Rubens*.

Hercules between Vice and Virtue, by *Jan Van den Hoecke*.

Portrait of Jean de Montfort, by *Anthonis Van Dyck*.

Although Van Dyck was apprenticed to and worked with Rubens, his style, especially in portraits, is quite different. His life is a kind of echo, in a minor key, of his magnificent master's. He was born in Antwerp in 1599 into a rich local family. In 1615, he already had his own workshop. In 1620, he had his first great chance, when he was appointed Rubens' chief assistant in the project of frescoing the church of San Carlo Borromeo. The same year he was invited to move to London and was offered an annual salary of 100 pounds. In Anglican England, religious themes were out of bounds, so Antonis was able to give his favourite bent full rein: portrait painting. In 1621 he made his way for the first time to Italy: he went to Genoa, where he painted a magnificent series of full-length portraits for the patrician families of the town. He then travelled on to Florence, Rome, Bologna and Venice (where Titian's innovations exercised a marked effect on his style). In 1624 he was invited by the Viceroy Emanuele Filiberto of Savoy to Palermo. A few months later, he fled, to escape from an epidemic of the plague. He had become the most renowned portrait painter in Europe: the courts of Brussels and London vying with each other for his services. He opted for England (and for a very desirable knighthood), even if he did not give-up travelling completely. «Sir Anthony van Dyke» died in London on the 9th December 1641, in his beautiful house in Blackfriars, that had been given to him by the King. A brief, intense life, richly gratified throughout by the great success he had earned through his extraordinary capacity and precocious talent. Upon this point, a historian of his time – one Giovanni Pietro Bellori – relates that Rubens, who was generously protective towards most of his young pupils, was vaguely jealous of the noticeable qualities of his very young follower, and was the first to direct the latter's efforts towards portrait-painting, so that he would not become a dangerous competitor in the other painting fields, in which, he, Rubens, wished to be paramount in.

Above: **Portrait of Jean de Montfort, by Antonis van Dyck;** *below*: **Portrait of Marguerite of Lorraine, by Antonis van Dyck.**

Above: **Henri IV triumphantly entering Paris, by P.P. Rubens;** *below*: **Bacchanal, by P.P. Rubens and** (*right*) **The Cardinal Infante Ferdinand of Spain triumphantly entering Antwerp, by Jan van den Hoecke.**

ROOM 42
(the Niobe Room)

The Hellenistic group of Niobe and the Niobedes belonged to the architectural complex of the temple to Sosian Apollo, in Rome. After its discovery, it remained for years in the open in the gardens of the Roman Villa Medici. Between 1778 and 1787, the group was moved to Florence, by order of Grand Duke Peter Leopold (Hapsburg-Lorraine) and arranged in the room specially prepared for it in the Uffizi. The room was designed by Zanobi del Rosso and is in the neo-Classical style, decorated with gilded stucco and friezes illustrating the Niobe myth. According to Ovid's version, she was daughter to Tantalus and queen of Thebes and had born seven sons and seven daughters. Her materal pride had led her to boast about them to Leto, who had only given birth to Apollo and Artemis, who therefore avenged their mother's hurt pride by killing all Niobe's children.

Niobe and her children, Roman copies of 3rd-2nd century B.C. Hellenistic originals.

Medici vase, neo-Attic, (3rd-2nd century B.C.).

Rearing Horse, Roman.

ROOM 43
(Caravaggio)

Born in Caravaggio, on the 28th September 1573, he was apprenticed in Milan to Simone Peterzano. After several years of tough, disordered living, he managed to attract the attention of Cardinal Del Monte, who took him into his service. Powerful families, like the Colonna, the Massimo and the Barberini, as well as important personalities like the Marquis Giustiniani, Asdrubale Mattei and above-all Cardinal Scipione Borghese also start taking an interest in him. His difficult, quarrelsome nature was not exactly conducive to a quiet regular life-style. He was involved in brawls and duels and was taken to court and imprisoned more than once, but always let free thanks to the protection afforded to him by one of his many powerful patrons. On the 29th May 1606, following a brawl that broke out on a rackets court, he killed Tomassoni da Terni and fled for his life. His wanderings led him first to Naples, where he painted the Seven Works of Mercy *and other masterpieces. He then sailed to Malta, where he once again ended up in prison, after having had much success and many honours showered upon him. He escaped yet again, this time fleeing to Sicily. In 1609, he returned to Naples, where he decided to stay and wait for the pardon Cardinal Gonzaga was to grant him. In June 1610, he started on a sea-voyage, but left the ship in Porto Ercole, and shortly afterwards, consumed by a «malign fever» (malaria?), he died, aged 39.*

Sacrifice of Isaac, by Michelangelo Merisi, known as *Caravaggio*, c. 1590.

This work, painted in Rome for Cardinal Maffeo Barberini,

Above: **detail from an Arras, with Stories of Moses in the Niobe Room**; *below*: **detail of the Dance of the Cupids, by Francesco Albani.**

Overall view of the Niobe Room; *below*: Summer pastimes, by Guercino.

already reveals the revolutionary innovations introduced by Caravaggio into 17th century painting. Decidedly breaking away from the idealistic, magniloquent naturalism of his time, Caravaggio invented a new language of crude, dramatic realism, that no longer strove after ideal beauty, but depicted the realities of life. In this picture, he uses a direct beam of light, which travels from the angel's shoulders, along his arm to the poised hand of Abrham, spotlighting Isaac, already crouched in a desperate howl of terror, as the old man's brutal, violent gesture is blocked at the culminating point of the drama. Not even the peaceful Giorgionesque landscape in the background manages to attenuate the vibrant intensity of the scene.

Angel's Head, by *G.L. Bernini.*

Harbour with Villa Medici, by *Claude Lorrain*, 1667.

This is one of Claude Lorrain's magnificent imaginary landscapes. Typical of Lorrain's painting is the juxtaposition of architectural constructions and superb seascapes drenched in a golden hazy shimmer.

Man with a monkey, by *Annibale Carracci.*

The Young Bacchus, by Michelangelo Merisi known as *Caravaggio*, c. 1589.

This is a youthful work, painted just after the artist had moved to Rome from his hometown, Caravaggio, in Northern Italy, and he does not as yet use light, as he will later on, to add excitement to a scene by spotlighting part of the picture and leaving the rest in shadow. In this adolescent Bacchus the forms are not sharply focused and the light is quite uniform, yet several innovations are already evident. His model, first of all, is not an idealized god but an ordinary young Roman boy, depicted with candid naturalism. Secondly, the realistically rendered fruitbowl on the table is treated for the first time as a still-life, a subject which will continue to enjoy great popularity starting from the 17th century.

Landscape with figures, by *Salvator Rosa.*

Medusa, by Michelangelo Merisi known as *Caravaggio.*

This frightening image of the severed head of Medusa was painted on a leather jousting shield for Cardinal Francesco Maria del Monte sometime after 1590.

Vanity, by *Mattia Preti.*

Neptune pursuing Coronides, by *Giulio Carpioni.*

Annunciation, by *Simon Vouet.*

Dance of the cupids, by *Francesco Albani.*

Summer pastimes, by Giovanni Francesco Barbieri known as *Guercino.*

Bacchante, by *Annibale Carracci.*

Born in Bologna and a contemporary of Caravaggio, Annibale conformed to the academic canons of religious painting, but adopted a profoundly poetic language.

Above: **Annunciation, by Simon Vouet,** *below*: **Landscape with figures, by Salvator Rosa.**

Above: **Sacrifice of Isaac**; *below*: **Medusa head and the Young Bacchus, three splendid works by Michelangelo Merisi, known as Caravaggio.**

ROOM 44
(Rembrandt, the Flemish and Dutch Masters)

In the 17th century, two very diverse artistic trends developed within a fairly restricted area. Rubens' courtly style flourished in the Catholic part of Flanders occupied by Spain under Albert and Isabella at the same time as Rembrandt's bourgeois style prospered in Calvinistic, democratic Netherlands. The numerous Dutch paintings of the time were commissioned by Protestant burghers for their dwellings. The most frequent themes are scenes from everyday life: landscapes, still-lives, portraits, interiors. Myths, historical subjects or Biblical episodes are much more rare. From a stylistic viewpoint, the artists attempt as realistic a style as possible in representing their subjects in un-heroic, un-solemn, natural poses. Later, when a new aristocracy started emerging in the Netherlands, the Classical Academism, prevalent in the rest of Europe started making itself felt in Dutch painting too. Initially, however a painter only had to contend with the requirements of a varied, favourably disposed market that viewed paintings as an excellent form of investment. Displeasing consequences will not be lacking, however, as Rembrandt himself was to find out: the enormous number of paintings on offer causing prices to drop, forcing many artists to seek alternative employment or risk total penury. Thus van de Velde opened a draper's shop, Hobbema became a tax-collector and Jan Steen ran a tavern.

Above: **Portrait of an old man, by Rembrandt van Rijn;** *below*: **the Huntsman and the lady, by Gabriel Metsu.**

Conversation, by *Peter Codde*.

Concert, by *Peter Codde*.

Hilly Landscape, by *Hercules Seghers*.

Copper mine, by Herri met de Bles known as *Civetta*.

The Charlatan, by *Frans Van Mieris*.

Mercury and Erse, by *Jacob Pynas*.

Scullery Maid, by *Caspar Netscher*.

The Painter's family, by *Frans Van Mieris*.

Peasants in an inn, by *Jan Miense Molenaer*.

The artist as a young man, by *Rembrandt*, c. 1634.

Portrait of an old man, by *Rembrandt van Rijn*.

The artist as an old man, by *Rembrandt van Rijn*, c. 1664. Rembrandt was influenced by Caravaggio and the Venetian school as his emphatic use of light and shade effects and his rich, warm palette reveals. Painted in rapid decisive strokes, his portraits reveal deep psychological insights.

Pygmalion and Galatea, by *Godfrey Schalcken*.

Landscape, by *Cornelis van Poelenburgh*.

The Miser, by *Hendrick Guerritsz Pot*.

Rest after the chase, by *Johannes Lingelbach*.

Above: **Landscape with huntsmen, by Paul Bril;** *below*: **Self-portraits of the artist as an old man (***and right***) as a young man, by Rembrandt van Rijn.**

The Repast, by *Jan Steen*.

Still life with fruit, insects and a lizard, by *Rachel Ruysch*.

Rachel Ruysch, a Dutchwoman, born in Amsterdam (1664-1756), was one of the many painters who chose to limit her production to a specialized field (a practice frequently adopted throughout the 17th century). She hardly ever painted anything other than fruit or flowers, which she portrayed with painstaking technical perfection and elegance. The term «Still-life» was used for the first time towards the middle of the 17th century, to indicate anything that was not «alive» (unlike the historical, religious or mythological scenes which were reccomended by the Academies as forms of «superior» art). The term adopted by the Anglo-Saxon countries was less derogatory than the Italian term («natura morta» = «dead nature») and more of a reference to still, silent immobility (Still-leven in Dutch, Still-leben in German, Still-life in English). Antiquity offers us many still-lives: all of them generally included within more extensive decorative schemes, but the still-life genre only emerged properly in the 17th century. In the 16th/17th centuries the so-called «vanitas» type of compositions which were basically still-lives, containing symbolic, allegorical-allusive elements stressing the transient nature of everything material established itself. Even in an unreligious context, however, the flower and fruit compositions gradually took a leading rôle, the «real» subject being used as a mere pretext and pushed right to the back of the picture.

Lady playing the lute, by *Cornelis Bega*.

The Huntsman and the Lady, by *Gabriel Metsu*.

Landscape with huntsmen, by *Paul Bril*.

Paul, from Antwerp, like his brother Mattheus, was very active in Italy, specially in Rome. Paul was probably the most gifted of the two, to such an extent that, although younger than his brother, he is often considered his master. They were both landscapists and had a noticeable influence on Roman artists of the time.

The Groote Markt of Haarlem, by *Gerrit Adriaensz Berckheyde*.

Vase of flowers, by *Jan van Huysum*.

Old couple at their meal, by *F. van Mieris the Elder*.

Landscape, by *Jan Both*.

Landscape with ford, by *Jan Breughel the Elder*.

Landscape, by *Jacob van Ruysdael*.

Born in Haarlem, in 1628, the artist later moved to Amsterdam; Salomon, an uncle of his was a successful landscapist. Jacob gave early proof of his talent in landscapes painted with considerable technical ability. He disregarded all academic formulae and endeavoured to represent reality in a fashion that revealed his profound knowledge of nature. He was also a practicing physician and barber.

Above: **Scullery Maid, by Caspar Netscher**; *below*: **an Old Couple at their Meal, by Frans van Mieris the Elder.**

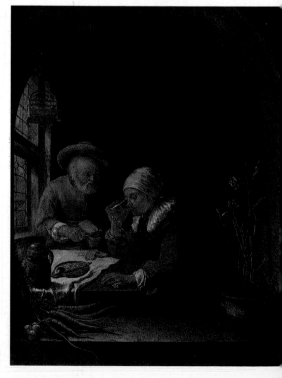

Above: **Still life with fruit, insects and a lizard, by Rachel Ruysch;**
below: **Peasants in an inn, by Jan Miense Molenaer.**

ROOM 45
(Eighteenth century painting)

Among the many 18th century Italian and non-Italian painters represented in this room, the most remarkable visual impact is provided by the Venetian landscapists and by Goya. The latter was born in Fuendetodos, near Saragossa, on the 30th March 1746. He grew up under the influence of the eclectic culture of the court, inspired by the teachings of Mengs. At the end of the 18th century, he was appointed «pintor del Rey» and «pintor de Camara» and became the official portrait painter of the royal family. His style was in the meantime developing along new lines. He moved away from the naturalistic trend and entered a fully Romantic dimension of dreamlike, visionary figures, which peaks in his disquieting Caprichos (1796-98). *The dramatic effects of the Napoleonic invasion, tenaciously opposed by the Spaniards, were powerfully expressed in the cycle known as the* Desastres de la guerra. *The repressive climate that ensued after the restauration of Ferdinand VII in 1823, obliged Goya to flee the country. In 1824 he left Madrid for Bordeaux, where he died shortly afterwards, in 1828.*

Portrait of the Countess of Chinchon's mother on horseback, by *Francisco Goya Lucientes.*

These two Goya portraits are splendid examples of the great Spaniard's skill in rendering his sitters' psychological reality. An unconventional figure, Goya rejected the codified academic canons of 18th century art, and painted according to his own ideas, seeking complete artistic freedom. His delicate luminous palette and painterly style convey great force and intensity.

Maria Theresa of Bourbon and Vallabriga, Countess of Chinchon, by *Francisco Goya Lucientes.*

Girl with a shuttle-cock, by *Jean Baptiste Chardin.*

Born into a fairly simple family (his father was a cabinet maker), Jean Baptiste had to give up the literary studies he would have liked to pursue. A famous engraver of his time, Cochin, relates a tasty anecdote: in order to get a proper estimate regarding the value of his first paintings, Chardin had summoned a small crowd of art-lovers to whom he had then exhibited his own as well as other painters' works. The result was, on the whole, fairly satisfactory: the onlookers seem to have opined that his pictures had been painted by a «good Flemish master». His works, copied extensively by himself and by able engravers, rapidly achieved enormous success, selling both to a large group of aristrocratic art-lovers, as well as to a wider and less select clientèle. His favourite subjects were simple, quiet representations of everyday bourgeois life. Portraits, still-lives are some of his most frequent subjects and his apparently facile brush ably masks a masterly accurate technique.

Boy playing with cards, by *Jean Baptiste Chardin.*

Putting up a statue of the Emperor, by *Giovan Battista Tiepolo,* c. 1726.

Flora, by *Rosalba Carriera.*

Above: **M. Theresa de Bourbon y Vallabriga, Countess of Chinchon, by F. Goya;** *below*: **Girl with shuttlecock, by J.B. Chardin.**

Above: **View of the San Marco wharf, by Canaletto;** *below*: **the Flea, by Giuseppe Maria Crespi and**
(*right***) Boy playing with cards, by J.B. Chardin.**

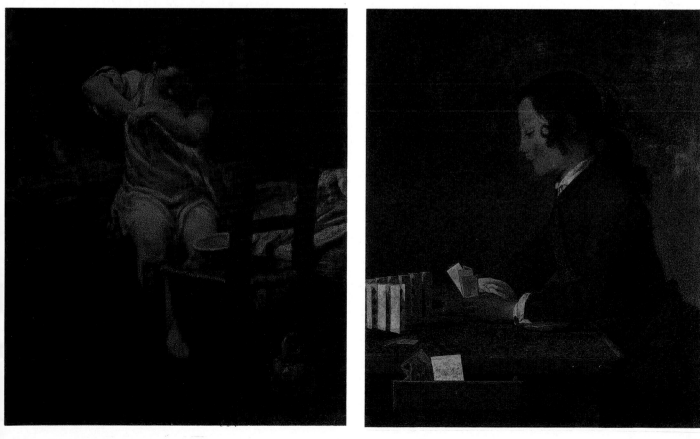

View of the San Marco wharf, by *Antonio Canal* or *Canaletto*.

Portrait of a lady, by *Alessandro Longhi*.

View of the Canal Grande from the Rialto Bridge, by Antonio Canal known as *Canaletto*.

The Venetian masters Canaletto and Guardi were the foremost painters of «*vedutismo*» (landscapism) which was highly fashionable throughout the 18th century. Canaletto's art is characterized by perfect perspective, crystal-clear atmospheres, cold colour - in short, he achieves an objective, photographic reconstruction of reality. His favorite subjects were views of Venice in which each tiny detail is lovingly rendered so that it becomes part of an organic, rational representation of reality.

Seascape with an arch, by *Francesco Guardi*.

Village with a canal, by *Francesco Guardi*.

Guardi's approach to landscape differs from Canaletto's, although in many ways they are similar. Guardi treats reality with a bit more immagination and sentiment. Also, he used thick dabs of pigment in comparison to Canaletto's smoother surfaces, and his palette is much more subtle.

The Confession, by *Pietro Longhi*.

Susanna and the Old Men, by *G.B. Piazzetta*.

The Flea, by *Giuseppe Maria Crespi*.

The Bolognese School, after the Carracci, managed throughout the 17th century, to maintain a high professional and artistic level. The accent was on decorative painting, with the many «specialisations» that this choice involved, such as scenographic or trompe l'oeil techniques. Giuseppa Maria Crespi's study of the great masters, with especial reference to Guercino and Carracci, was carried out with passionate conviction and an animatedly religious and moralistic spirit. After being attracted by the decorative genre he moved on almost immediately towards other fields, such as still-lives and everyday scenes, that he depicted attentively recording minute episodes and seemingly negligible objects of everyday life. He adopted the same courageously attentive viewpoint when engaged in religious subjects.

The Painter's family, by *Giuseppe Maria Crespi*.

Portrait of Vittorio Alfieri, by *Xavier Fabre*.

Portrait of the Countess of Albany, by *Xavier Fabre*.

Portrait of Marie Adelaide of France, by *Jean Marc Nattier*.

Portrait of Marie Zephyrine of France, by *Jean Marc Nattier*.

Portrait of Marie Adelaide of France in Turkish dress, by *Etienne Liotard*, 1753.

Portrait of Marie Henriette of France as Flora, by *Jean Marc Nattier*.

Above: **Putting up a statue of the Emperor, by G.B. Tiepolo;** *below*: **Portrait of Marie Zephyrine of France, by J.M. Nattier.**

Above: **Portrait of Marie Henriette of France, as Flora, by J.M. Nattier;** *below*: **Portrait of Vittorio Alfieri, by Xavier Fabre** (*and right*) **Portrait of the Countess of Chinchon's mother on horseback, by F. Goya.**

INDEX OF THE ARTISTS

INDEX